EDITH HAMILTON
An Intimate Portrait

Books by Edith Hamilton

THE GREEK WAY, *1930* (*Revised, 1942*)

THE ROMAN WAY, *1932*

THREE GREEK PLAYS, *1937*

MYTHOLOGY, *1942*

WITNESS TO THE TRUTH (*Revised, 1957*)

SPOKESMEN FOR GOD, *1949*

THE ECHO OF GREECE, *1957*

THE COLLECTED DIALOGUES OF PLATO
(*Edited by Edith Hamilton and Huntington Cairns, 1961*)

THE EVER-PRESENT PAST, *1964*

EDITH HAMILTON

An Intimate Portrait

BY

DORIS FIELDING REID

W · W · NORTON & COMPANY · INC ·
New York

FIRST EDITION

Library of Congress catalog card no. 67-12449. Published simultaneously in Canada by George J. McLeod Limited, Toronto. Printed in the United States of America.

1 2 3 4 5 6 7 8 9 0

To Alice Hamilton

"She was balm to my soul."

E. H.

Contents

🦫 Illustrations appear between pages 96 and 97

Publisher's Note

⇝ TO bring out over a period of three decades the works of an author whom one also counts as a friend is one of the rich and rewarding experiences of serving as publisher.

Throughout the years our relationship with Edith Hamilton was unique. It was a relationship of trust, of mutual understanding and respect. We literally had to badger her into accepting the necessary formalities of the business. She never wrote a business letter. Her letters were always personal. She never made copies of them, and she usually destroyed the letters that came to her.

For this reason and because all the letters and documents of her earlier years disappeared in a disastrous Connecticut River flood in 1938, no conventional biography of this great lady, whose books have been keenly appreciated by millions of readers, could be written. So we turned to her closest friend to write of Edith Hamilton's life.

Doris Fielding Reid inherited an intimate family relationship. She first knew Miss Hamilton in her parents' home in Baltimore. She was likewise her pupil at the Bryn Mawr School. Following Miss Hamilton's retire-

ment and throughout the subsequent forty years they shared a home, first in New York, later in Washington, with summers always spent at Sea Wall on Mt. Desert Island, Maine. Doris Reid knew Edith Hamilton in her day-to-day life as no one else did. And Miss Hamilton, from her side, appreciated Miss Reid's clear intelligence and judgment in much lively discussion of her writings. For every good reason she dedicated her famous first book, The Greek Way, *to Doris Reid.*

Miss Reid has drawn on her own special knowledge and memory as well as on the memory of those friends who were privileged to know Edith Hamilton well. She has presented a portrait which no one else could possibly have managed to write.

Acknowledgments

❧ I MUST EXPRESS *my appreciation for the help I have received in writing this book. Edith Hamilton never kept a diary of any kind and she had little or no interest in reminiscing.*

I am therefore particularly indebted to the close friends that she made in New York and Washington who told me, or reminded me, of stories about her and of their visits with her, or who sent me the letters she had written to them over a period of many years, as well as to some Baltimoreans who had gone through the Bryn Mawr School while Edith was headmistress.

Among those, not specifically named but whom I have often quoted, are Mr. and Mrs. Raymond Baldwin, Mrs. Hamilton Bryan, Mr. and Mrs. John Clendenin, Mr. and Mrs. Daniel Crena de Iongh, Mr. and Mrs. Charles House, Mrs. Seth Milliken, Mr. and Mrs. Felix Morley, Mr. Vail Motter, Mr. Herbert Schaumann, Mr. George Stevens, Mr. and Mrs. Alan Valentine, Gen. and Mrs. Albert Wedemeyer, Mr. John White, Dr. and Mrs. Arnold Wolfers, and many more. I am immeasurably grateful to them all.   Doris Fielding Reid
Sea Wall, Maine

EDITH HAMILTON
An Intimate Portrait

Childhood in Fort Wayne

⟡A BIOGRAPHY—practically all biographies—must of necessity be written in the past tense. A biography of Edith Hamilton, therefore, will seem somehow unreal for quite a while to come. Shortly after her death an acquaintance wrote me, "I can imagine Edith Hamilton in any number of circumstances but I cannot conceive of her as dead." This same reaction has been expressed by many people.

Her extraordinary power and vitality of mind and body made it seem in no way surprising that she should write her introductions to the Dialogues of Plato after her ninety-second birthday. Her keenness of mind, her wit—"she was such fun" one said to me—her intensity affected all who knew her. It is hardly an exaggeration to say that no one who met her ever forgot her. Where this swift spirit has gone, I do not know; but to those she cared for on this earth she brought life.

In her autobiography, *Exploring Dangerous Trades* (published by Atlantic Monthly Press in 1948), Edith's sister, Dr. Alice Hamilton, describes their forebears, tells whence they sprang, and gives some vivid pictures of their early life and education. As Alice was only eighteen months younger than Edith, their childhood environment was identical. Edith often said that Alice's account could not be improved upon.

It is very unusual to have available such material. Most biographies are written by persons who knew their subjects only in the latter part of their lives or who knew them personally not at all. I am very lucky to have Alice's authentic first-hand picture of where they lived and how. I shall draw heavily on this material.

Edith Hamilton was born on August 12, 1867. Her mother had gone to Germany to be with her relatives who were living there at that time, and Edith was born in Dresden. She was barely two months old when Mrs. Hamilton returned with her baby to the United States, and little did her parents realize that, as the years rolled on, the trivial accident of Edith's place of birth would result in time-consuming conversations with practically everyone in the passport division of our State Department and elsewhere around the world and that she would sometimes be introduced on lecture platforms as of "German descent." Nothing could be further from the truth.

In a letter from an old friend he writes, "I have a clear and vivid memory of Edith's account of her great grandfather who emigrated to Canada.

"He was the youngest son of the Abercorn branch of the Hamilton family. The family occupied a sizeable mansion on a great estate in North Ireland. This great grandfather of Edith's, realizing that as the youngest son he would not inherit any sizeable patrimony, took his chances and emigrated to Canada. In Canada, by reason of his gentle and genteel upbringing and because of his small and delicate hands, he was unable to find work in that then frontier world of Canada. After considerable discouragement he at last got a job as a deck hand on the flatboats that were used on the wilderness canals. On one such trip the destination was the Indian outpost, Fort Wayne, Indiana. For some reason or other he jumped ship, so to speak, and settled there. Land was cheap and he invested in land on which later much of the city of Fort Wayne was built. This, as with the case of John Jacob Astor and New York, was the source of a very considerable fortune.

"And it was this fortune which enabled the great grandfather to give to his children, one of them being Edith's grandfather, the advantages of education and travel which the great grandfather had been denied."

Her grandfather, Allen Hamilton, also came over from the North of Ireland as a young man and joined his father, who had settled in Fort Wayne, Indiana. This little city became Edith's and her sisters' childhood home and her generation was the fourth to live there.

Edith's childhood environment and education were most unusual. She was the eldest of four sisters who were born within a six-year period. During the first few years of her life she, with her three younger sisters, lived in their grandfather's house, which they always referred to as The Old House. It was built on some ten acres of land in the middle of the town of Fort Wayne. Her father, Montgomery Hamilton, and her uncle, Andrew Holman Hamilton, subsequently built their own houses on the same big place. There were eleven cousins of Edith's generation, eight of whom were near enough in age to play together, and, in spite of the fact that they were not sent to school, they felt no need of associations outside of the family, no desire for what Edith always referred to as "outsiders." An unmarried aunt, their father's sister, also lived there in The Old House and Edith's childhood was spent surrounded by "the Hamiltons." One wonders how Edith's mother and Andrew Hamilton's wife managed. They were not Hamiltons! Be that as it may, Edith, her sisters, and her cousins developed an intimacy in their early childhood which lasted throughout their long lives.

Of their grandfather's house and their house Alice wrote: "Our Hamilton grandfather's house was large and substantial. It was of brick and had been built in 1840 with three stories and a two-storied ell and a basement kitchen. Like most houses of a hundred years ago, it was built for beauty, space, dignity, not for comfort and convenience. The ceilings were fourteen feet high, the rooms were spacious, and a wood-burning furnace made little impression on the cold of our Indiana winter. There were open fires in every room. Nobody thought of the endless carrying of wood, coal, ashes, up and down the long stairways, for there was always a 'hired man' who had little else to do in winter. There were also plenty of housemaids to carry clean water upstairs and dirty water downstairs in those preplumbing days.

"On top of the house was what we called the 'cupola,' a square little room, big enough for a crowd of us and never disturbed by the grownups. To reach it we passed a forbidden door which led into a room we were told had no floor. It was a horrible thought, that bottomless pit of darkness, and we never ventured to turn the handle.

"Our frame house was the White House, our uncle's in the same grounds was the Red House, and of brick. Neither was so big as The Old House, and the ceilings were somewhat lower; the furnaces burned coal, and there was running water and a bathroom, so much had comfort progressed between 1840 and 1873. But space and dignity were still the first desiderata. Our hall was vast, and the rooms—library, parlor, dining room— opened into it by triple doors of black walnut, but as the hall could never be heated in winter, those doors had to be kept shut. The wide stairs were also black walnut. Of a winter's night, when the house was very still, a ghost might start at the attic door and come creaking down the two flights to the hall. This happened one evening when I was quite alone in the library, reading the fearsome tale of black magic in *The Lay of the Last Minstrel*."

Alice gives the following account of their ancestors: "Allen Hamilton came to Fort Wayne when it was still very primitive, an outpost in a land of Indians. His career was typical of America in those days. He dealt with Indians at first, and the tales that have come down to us show that his fairness won their confidence and respect. He played an important part in the development of the city and was one of a small group of men who put through the Pittsburgh, Fort Wayne & Chicago Railroad. He was ambitious for his family, sending his sons not only to college but to Göttingen and Jena Universities and his daughters to Miss Porter's School in Farmington, Connecticut. He was Scotch-Irish and my father always stressed the first word, but we children were fascinated by the Irish part and loved to hear tales of an old Irish Katy who came over with the family and who saw fairies and heard the banshee wail when our grandfather died.

"He found his bride, Emerine Jane Holman, in Aurora, an older, more settled community on the Ohio River not far from Cincinnati. She was only seventeen when she went with her young husband to that distant spot, Fort Wayne, where somehow she learned to preside over a large household and where she bore eleven children. The first four years of my life were spent in that house; and although after that we lived in a house of our own, it was on the same big place and The Old House with its orchard and cow pasture and extensive 'yard' (nobody had 'grounds' in those days) was as important a background for our lives as our own place. Our grandfather died before any of the younger generation were born, but our grandmother lived on till we older ones were in our teens. She was descended from English emigrants who settled first in Virginia, then moved on to Kentucky and to Southern Indiana.

"Our grandmother was a fascinating person to all of us, but we never knew her intimately; there was something elusive about her; and her affection, which embraced all seventeen of us cousins, was quite impersonal. She was a tiny person, quick and wiry, and her mind was as quick as her body. She loved reading, passionately. I can remember often seeing her in the library of The Old House, crouched over the fireplace where the soft coal fire had gone out without her knowing it, so deep had she been in her book. Once she was perched on top of a ladder, level with the last shelf of the bookcase. She had meant to dust the books but had come upon one so fascinating that she lost herself in it and forgot where she was. She could enthrall us children with Scott's poems, telling us the story in prose and suddenly dropping into long passages of the poetry, as for instance, the trial and walling up of Constance de Beverly in the monastery of Lindisfarne from *Marmion*.

"Our mother's father, Loyal Sylvester Pond, came from Vermont to New York and was a sugar importer dealing with Cuba chiefly. He died when I was still a child and I only remember him as white-haired, with very bright blue eyes and something about him which did not encourage real intimacy. My grandmother lived to a great age and played a large part in our lives. She was of Dutch descent, with English and Irish admixture, but to us, steeped as we were in Motley's Dutch Republic, the Dutch part of our ancestry was much the most interesting. Her education was typical of Mid-Victorianism and so was her outlook on life. She had gone to Miss Lucy Green's School in New York, where she had learned the most correct morals and manners, where she had come to adore Byron but had promised Miss Lucy never to read *Don Juan*, where her belief in the literal inspiration of the Bible and the complete iniquity of the Roman Catholic Church had been strengthened so that she never lost it, and her attitude toward social questions might be summed up by two statements I remember her making in later years. One was on the question of Negro slavery. 'Doubtless it was hard on the slaves, but we had to have cotton.' Another was on Lincoln. 'My dear, what was the name of our President during the war, a most uncouth person I always heard, though well-meaning in his way?' "

Edith's father, Montgomery Hamilton, was a man of means. He never had a profession and spent most of his time in his library reading. He took an interest in his first two daughters, Edith and Alice, and had definite ideas about what they should learn and how. His enthusiasms were for Macaulay, Froude, Addison, Scott, and Pope. He had little use for the New England writers, as he thought them unclear and muddled. He objected to the public schools—there were none other in Fort Wayne —because they taught too much arithmetic and American history, and he had no interest in either subject. He read them Macaulay's *Lays* and Scott's poems. Edith learned the whole of *The Lady of the Lake* by heart. She also learned pages of prose. Mr. Hamilton thought Addison and Sir Thomas Browne would develop her taste and style. She could quote passages from them all her life, but certainly they did not influence her style. Nothing could be less like Edith's style in writing than that of Sir Thomas Browne.

Mr. Hamilton was not a religious man but Alice writes that he "had a passion for Theology. There was a time when we knew more about Arianism, Socinianism, Gnosticism, and other heresies than we knew about the history of our own country. He insisted that Edith and I learn the Westminster Catechism, and many a struggle we had over that heathenish production." Edith often quoted to me these lines from it: "All mankind by Adam's fall lost communion with God, are under His wrath and curse, and so made liable to all the ills of this life, to death, and to the pains of Hell forever." She would laugh over it and say, "Imagine Socrates talking like that." But in her childhood she said it was a horror to her.

At a very early age Mr. Hamilton taught her Latin. "He was the world's worst teacher," Edith often said to me with amusement. As a starter he gave her a book called *Six Weeks Preparation for Caesar*. When Edith would ask him a question he could not answer, he would tell her to look it up in the *Encyclopedia Britannica*. He was interested in and had theories about the doctrine of the Trinity and told Edith to do some reading and find out what proof there was for it. When Alice told him that she wanted to be taught physics, he said she could teach herself. It was all in the encyclopedia.

Their mother had quite different ideas. She wanted the children to spend most of the day playing out of doors and to learn languages. She talked French to them when they were little and had them take French lessons later on. They learned German first from their servants, who were always German, and then from a Lutheran school teacher. This was the only formal teaching they had. Other subjects they had to learn themselves by reading, and, astonishingly, they did. Edith was a born reader from earliest childhood throughout her life. Alice was not, but she says that "family pressure" made her into a bookworm also. Most of the hours they were indoors were spent over books.

It was a truly remarkable family. When Edith talked of her childhood, she rarely said "I" or "I felt." It was always "we." And Alice, in her autobiography, rarely uses the word "I." She almost always writes "we" or "they." Edith's close, lifelong association with her sisters makes a word about them very much to the point.

They were very different types of persons, but they had these things in common: they were able, they were true intellectuals, and they had a breadth of culture beyond that of any other family I have known.

Alice went into medicine and got her M.D. in 1893 at Ann Arbor. She devoted herself to industrial diseases and made the subject of such importance that Harvard created a chair of industrial medicine and in 1919 asked Alice to occupy it. She was the first woman ever appointed to the Harvard faculty.

The third sister, Margaret, was head of the primary department of the Bryn Mawr School when Edith was headmistress. After Edith retired, Margaret subsequently became the highly successful head of the school.

Norah was six years younger than Edith and played considerably less part in her life than Alice and Margaret. At an early age she showed real talent for drawing. Alice's autobiography is illustrated with some of her striking etchings.

Years later—eighteen years after Edith was born— the Hamiltons had their first son, Arthur. An old German gentleman said to their father, "You should call your son Primus, Mr. Hamilton." But the sisters, who were all good feminists, said, "No indeed, he is only Quintus," and Quint he has been ever since. He, however, like his sisters, made his mark. He became an outstanding professor of Romance languages at the University of Illinois.

In Edith's generation parents did not play the active part in their children's lives that they do nowadays. In talking of her childhood, Edith always referred to her parents as the "grownups," from whom they got away as much as possible. In fact, the "grownups" did not concern themselves with their children's games and play. That was the children's responsibility, and they com-

posed long, continuing games: Robin Hood and His
Band, the Knights of the Round Table, the Siege of
Troy, with their carriage house as Troy and their wood
shed the Greek camp. Edith has often told me of the
tournaments they played with wooden swords, modeled
after the Knights of the Round Table. They did not put
out each other's eyes, which can be explained only by
the indestructibility of children generally. "Once we
were out of doors, we were free," writes Alice, "except
for a few prohibitions which we observed. We told the
truth but not always the whole truth because we argued
that the less the impulsive and incalculable grownups
knew, the better for them and us."

Their father's family was Presbyterian and the children all went to the First Presbyterian Church. From
Edith's description the service was plain and uninspiring
and the sermons long, but she looked back on her Sun-
days with pleasure. The day was entirely different from
weekdays. Breakfast, dinner, and supper, although exactly the same every Sunday, were quite different from
weekday meals. They read what Edith referred to as
"Sunday" books. The church was of interest partly because it constituted their rare excursions into the "outside world," which meant leaving the Hamilton
property.

Christmas was altogether different. The German
maids would wake the children at five-thirty, and after a
glass of milk in the kitchen they would steal out into the
dark winter morning, accompanied by an elderly Ger-

man manservant and a much-loved German nursemaid, and go over to the German Lutheran Church. It was brilliantly lighted, with great Christmas trees on either side of the altar. There was a simple sermon in German addressed to the children and then the classes from the Lutheran Schools sang such Christmas hymns as *"Uns ist ein Kind geboren"* and *"Ihr Kinderlein kommet."* When the service was over, they would follow the congregation up the streets in the German section of Fort Wayne to see the little lighted Christmas trees in every window. Edith often talked of these Christmases and how much she loved them.

Edith's mother was an Episcopalian and from her Edith learned the Psalms, the Sermon on the Mount, and the first chapter of St. John. In the summers they went to the little Episcopalian Church on Mackinac Island in Lake Michigan where, Alice writes, "we were steeped in the collects and the Litany and the Te Deum until they became part of us. The Bible was more familiar to us than any other book." In the last years of her life Edith often commented on modern education which brought up children with no knowledge of the Bible.

In their early childhood the Hamilton children spent their summers at the Old Sweet Springs in West Virginia. When Edith was about eleven they began to go to Mackinac Island, where their Hamilton grandmother had gone with her own children years before. Subsequently Edith's parents built a summer cottage there and they went to the island every summer for many years, until long after they were all grown up. As children, Edith and Alice would go out for several days in their father's sailboat on his fishing expeditions. The beauty of the Great Lakes, the moon on the water, the sound of the lapping waves entered into Edith's soul. She would speak of their swimming and picnicking, but in later years she never cared much for either. The beauties of nature and long walks were her greatest source of happiness from an early age throughout her life. Alice describes the passion of anticipation they both felt when the steamer that took them to Mackinac for their summer holiday drew near the island.

Edith talked very little about her personal feelings and reactions during her childhood—or at any other time, for that matter. Nonetheless a few things came through. She told me that she was very irritable as a child. She said, "They all irritated me occasionally beyond endurance, with the sole exception of Alice. She never irritated me. She was balm to my soul."

One of Edith's outstanding qualities all her life was her power to care. Once when Alice was a small child, she became very ill. Their mother would not let Edith go into Alice's room and Edith spent hours in misery on the floor outside the door.

As Edith grew older and felt she had outgrown the games of the younger children, she linked up with an older cousin, Jessie Hamilton, with whom she formed a deep and lasting friendship. They would sit up in a big apple tree or on the rafters of the carriage house reading and talking. When I would ask Edith what they discussed, she would just say, "Oh, everything. Books chiefly."

From earliest childhood throughout her life Edith had a phenomenal verbal memory. She was also a vivid and gifted storyteller. Alice writes: "Edith, the first born, though only eighteen months older than I, seemed much more mature, partly because she was a passionate reader while I was a reluctant one. Edith read everything she could lay her hands on. She was a natural storyteller, and on the long walks my mother insisted on our taking every day, Edith would give us résumés of Scott and Bulwer-Lytton and De Quincey. She could not understand my childish taste in books and she would stop at an exciting spot, such as Amy Robsart's death in *Kenilworth*, and say, 'Now you've got to finish it yourself.' Sometimes I did, but sometimes I slipped back to the 'Katy' books, to her infinite disgust. She also loved to learn poetry by heart, and as we walked to and from our daily music lesson, she would recite to me Macaulay's *Lays of Ancient Rome*, "Naseby," and "Ivry" till I knew them by heart. Then came Shelley, Keats, and Byron. I am sure I learned 'The Eve of St. Agnes' just by listening to her recite it."

Once Edith, after having read De Quincey's horror story, *The Avenger*, told it so vividly to the other children that Margaret said it haunted her for years and she dreaded to go into the clothes closet for fear she would discover a man's boots coming out from behind the dresses. Decades later I remember Edith telling stories to some children who listened in breathless silence with their eyes almost popping out of their heads.

While most of us can remember some person or persons who inspired us—who opened doors—I do not think this was ever the case with Edith. Her passion for the classics was in spite of, rather than because of, her father. Her inspirations came from the impact of what she read on her own original and gifted mind. Her cousin Jessie wrote me that she would always remember Edith at the age of thirteen combing her hair and reading a book written in Greek that lay open on her dresser.

Edith, as a child, absorbed and remembered an enormous amount of literature, but the impression that Greece and its poets made on her keenly receptive mind went deepest. It absorbed her from an incredibly early age and lasted throughout her life. I think most young people who have such a passionate absorption and are truly gifted have a notion in their early life as to what they are going to do and what they want to be. Edith never did. That she became a headmistress was in a sense a happen-chance. If anyone had told her she would later become one of the most distinguished literary figures and classicists of our time, she would quite simply have thought that person insane.

Temperamentally, Alice operated on an even keel. Edith was high strung and emotional. In a letter I have from Alice, she writes: "Edith had intense emotions which sometimes puzzled and distressed my matter-of-fact disposition. I remember a gloomy day in Mackinac when she and I stood looking out over a dark, stormy lake and heavy clouds. She must have been about 14 years old then. To my surprise she suddenly intoned, '*Grau wie der Himmel liegt vor mir die Welt.*' (Gray as the sky the world lies before me.) 'Oh, dear,' I said, 'you don't really feel like that?' 'Most of the time I do,' she answered. She had her times of joyous gaiety over the beauties of the outside world or a new book or some amusing family episode, but she had sudden deep depressions that mystified me."

Attendance at Miss Porter's School in Farmington, Connecticut, was a tradition in the Hamilton family. Three of Edith's aunts had been sent there, and then came the next generation—Edith, her sisters, and her cousins. All in all, ten of the Hamilton girls went to Farmington as they reached the ages of sixteen or seventeen. They all loved it, but none of them could explain exactly why. Alice wrote: "It is hard to make anyone who is not an old Farmington girl understand the love and loyalty we hold for Miss Porter's School, for some of the teaching we received was the world's worst." As Farmington was the first school Edith had ever attended, I once asked her how it struck her and what was she taught there. "Oh, we weren't *taught* anything," she answered. The courses were purely elective and if a girl was weak in any subjects, she could just decide not to take them.

Alice describes their course in mental and moral philosophy as consisting of memorizing paragraphs from textbooks and reciting them to an elderly German "who kept his eyes fixed on the ceiling, for he claimed that he knew the book by heart. There was never any discussion or explanation." One of the girls got the idea that mental philosophy might mean something and tried to puzzle out some ideas. The girls told her what a silly waste of time that was; the subject did not mean anything, and all she had to do was to learn the words by heart. "That was also all we had to do in the German literature class which was taught by the same gentleman."

On the other hand, Latin and Greek, German conversation, drawing, and music were well presented. The girls who did not elect to study music had the benefit of wonderful recitals by famous pianists. Old Professor Seymour, father of Charles Seymour, the former president of Yale, would come in the spring and lecture on Shakespeare and take over the Greek and Latin classes.

Edith often spoke of the pleasure she got from listening to Professor Seymour, but she never spoke of his having opened her eyes to this or that. She never made any comment of that kind. Perhaps her eyes were already opened. I do not know.

I have often heard Farmington referred to, with considerable condescension, as "a young ladies' finishing school." Edith did not look upon it in that way at all. It was Miss Porter herself and the atmosphere she created that made a lasting impression on Edith and on all the other Farmington girls with whom I have talked who were there when Miss Porter was its head. She was not only deeply cultured, but truly learned as well. She was quite disturbed, however, when Edith said she wanted to go to college, as she did not believe in college for girls. "My dear Edith, you can become learned," Edith quoted her as saying, "but, my dear Edith, I don't think much of learning."

Regardless of Miss Porter's point of view and the strenuous opposition of many members of Edith's family, she was determined to go to college and she chose Bryn Mawr. The Farmington curriculum was far from adequate to enable a girl to pass the entrance examinations, and when Edith graduated from the school she settled down at home to study. Among other subjects, she was required to take an examination in trigonometry. She knew practically no arithmetic, let alone trigonometry, so she bought a book, taught herself the subject, and passed the examination.

Bryn Mawr College and Germany

EDITH went through college in two years, concentrating on the classics, and won the European Fellowship. This was given by Bryn Mawr College to the outstanding student in its graduating class. It was a cash award to enable the winner to spend a year abroad studying in any country of her choosing.

Very little information is available about Edith's life and career at Bryn Mawr. All her early letters to her family from Farmington, Bryn Mawr, and, later, Germany, where she went with her sister Alice on the European Fellowship, were kept in the basement of her sisters' house at Hadlyme on the Connecticut River and were all washed away when the river flooded in the hurricane of 1938. This is an irreplaceable loss to a biographer.

Edith reminisced very little during her lifetime, all her contemporaries in college are dead, and Alice did not go to Bryn Mawr. One story, however, has come down of Edith's college days. Student government had been inaugurated when she got there and a rule had been made that any girl caught smoking would be expelled, and it was up to the girls to enforce the rule by reporting any culprit they came across. Edith thought this whole idea was scandalous. In the first place, she said, the rule was not important as smoking was not a crime, and in the second place, for girls to report one another was just "beneath contempt." She gathered groups of girls together and made speeches on the subject. She won the entire student body over to her side and the regulation was repealed. This tale was told me some years ago by one of her classmates. I cannot remember Edith's ever referring to it.

When she spoke of her college days it was always about her thrill when she won the European Fellowship. Her personality, vitality, and drive, however, must have registered with the college faculty because while she was in Germany the dean of Bryn Mawr, Miss M. Carey Thomas, wrote in 1896 offering her the post of headmistress of the Bryn Mawr School in Baltimore. Edith's reaction to this was very typical. She had never thought of becoming the head of a school and I am sure she had no desire to do so. For that matter she had never visualized any particular career for herself. But her father had lost his money and a job was wanted. Here was a job, and regardless of the fact that she knew nothing about teaching, let alone the running of a school, she accepted the challenge.

Edith's and Alice's year in Germany was interesting and rewarding. Alice had just received her M.D. from

Ann Arbor and was studying bacteriology and pathology. Edith, of course, was studying the classics. A 1965 article by Alice in the *Atlantic Monthly* dwells chiefly on the Germany of the 1890's and the Germans' attitude toward women at that time. She has, however, this to say concerning Edith's few months at the University of Leipzig: "Edith was deeply disappointed in her Greek and Latin courses. The lecturers were very thorough linguistically but most uninspiring. Instead of the grandeur and beauty of Aeschylus and Sophocles, it seemed that the important thing was their use of the second aorist."

The paragraph is illuminating. It seems that by that time Edith had realized what was and what was not important to her in her exhaustive study of the Greek language and the Greeks. The reasons for her lifetime convictions of the importance of ancient Greece were by then formulated. They had nothing to do with the use of the second aorist or the subjunctive, and the glamour and authority of the famous classicists at the University of Leipzig affected her not at all.

After a few months in Leipzig the two sisters went to Munich, where they found the university, the people, and the climate much more agreeable and stimulating.

Alice writes of Edith's entrance into the University of Munich: "Her admission to the University was a cause of such excitement among the students that a kind, elderly professor offered to see her through it on her first day. She assured him it would not be necessary, but was indeed grateful to him when she found the University Place crowded with students waiting to see the first woman go in. If a woman were admitted to lectures in the classical department, it would mean that a seminarian might have to sit next to her, even share a manuscript with her if there were not enough to go around. It was shocking even to think of it. All sorts of arrangements were suggested. I remember especially an ingenious one, that a little loge, a theater box, be built for her with curtains so that the seminarians could not even see her. Finally it came to a chair up on the lecturer's platform, where nobody could be contaminated by contact with her." Of course, one can hardly conceive of a plan that would have made her more conspicuous.

Edith often referred to this episode with great amusement. She wrote, "The head of the University used to stare at me, then shake his head and say sadly to a colleague, 'There, now you see what's happened? We're right in the midst of the woman question.'" She found the professors more interesting than those in Leipzig. Some, she said, were really kind to her. One in particular "treated me as if he actually liked having me there!" She intended to take her Ph.D. in Munich but then Miss Thomas' letter came and Edith returned to America to take over the Bryn Mawr School. I am sure she would have liked to continue her studies in Germany a little longer but, typically, she never seemed to care whether she had a Ph.D. or not.

The Bryn Mawr School, Baltimore

⸙ THE Bryn Mawr School was founded in Baltimore, Maryland, in 1885, the same year as the opening of Bryn Mawr College. In order to graduate from the school a girl was required to pass the Bryn Mawr College entrance examinations, and there was no alternative course. It was the only strictly college preparatory school for girls in the entire United States.

One could hardly think of a more unlikely place than Baltimore to start such an experiment. Baltimore was essentially a southern city, where girls were not supposed to learn anything in particular. There were in the city twenty-nine other small private schools for girls, most of them run by impoverished southern ladies. It was only twenty years after the Civil War. None of their pupils could possibly have passed a college examination, and their parents would have thought it most undesirable for them to do so. In fact, the whole idea was anathema to Baltimore parents, not only in 1885 but for some decades to come.

I was a pupil in the Bryn Mawr School from 1903 to

1911, and in that period one of Baltimore's leading gynecologists told Edith that he knew that women were so made that the study of Latin was bad for their health! Perhaps this belief was more excessive than that held by the average Baltimore parent, but it was a universal conviction that a real education would prevent a girl from getting a husband.

The school was founded by that redoubtable warrior, the first dean of Bryn Mawr College, Miss M. Carey Thomas. Why she decided to attempt this highly novel and experimental project in Baltimore can only be explained by the fact that she was herself a Baltimorean. Furthermore, her great friend, Miss Mary Garrett, who shared Miss Thomas' passion for the education of women and who had the wherewithal and the desire to put up a building for the school, belonged to that city.

Miss Garrett built the school in the heart of Baltimore on the corner of Cathedral and Preston streets. It was five stories high and there was an art room with northern light on the top floor. It had a science laboratory and a fully equipped gymnasium with a race track around the top and a swimming pool. There was no school building comparable to it in the 1880's or for many years to come. There were truly beautiful winding stairs with imported iron banisters, and Miss Garrett had brought plaster casts from Europe of various Greek statues, which were placed in the entrance hall. On the walls of the huge study hall, which seated the whole main school, was a reproduction of the Parthenon frieze.

The yellow bricks for the school house were also imported, and Miss Garrett is supposed to have climbed a ladder to make sure that the brick work was exactly correct. This may be a myth, but the story has come down through the years. When it was decided, in 1928, to move the school into the suburbs, a contractor told us laughingly that there would not be enough dynamite in Baltimore to blow it up. It still stands and is now called the Deutsches Haus and is used as a beer parlor.

The school had no headmistress for the first years. "Having been a headmistress myself," said Miss Thomas' niece, Millicent Carey McIntosh, "I can well understand why a school which insisted that girls should study Latin, which didn't allow them to drop subjects just because they didn't like them, preferred to have only a secretary who reported to Miss Thomas up in Bryn Mawr College. She, who was a hundred and twenty-five miles away, was safe from the rage of the parents."

The Bryn Mawr School was not taking hold, when, in the autumn of 1896, a train pulled into Baltimore carrying Edith Hamilton, who was to become its first headmistress. In her address at the 75th Anniversary of the school on November 4, 1960, she said: "I have been thinking a lot of the early days of the school. . . . I was very young and very ignorant when I first came to Baltimore and, I may say, very, very, frightened. I remember vividly saying to myself as I traveled down here, 'If I were put in charge of running this train, I could hardly know less how to do it than I know how to run the Bryn

Mawr School.' "

Edith was headmistress for twenty-six years, and when she retired in 1922 the Bryn Mawr School was the largest and far and away the most prominent and popular school for girls in Baltimore. In fact, by the time I got there it was *the* school for girls in the city. How did Edith achieve this? For, in addition to the allergy Baltimoreans had for the idea of education for girls, Edith had another big hurdle to take: she came from the North. It is difficult for anyone who is not a Baltimorean to grasp or even believe the attitude of Baltimore families at that time. It was not only that they thought old Baltimore southern families were the best, but they felt that no one else really mattered at all; and the embryo school was drawing chiefly from the families of those who did not "matter at all." Edith, as a new and very young headmistress, was given some kindly advice from thoughtful Baltimoreans to the effect that as the school was set up it would inevitably draw from this class alone.

Edith was determined that the school should grow and become an effectual part of the city. How did she accomplish this? There are many explanations but one not so often recognized is mentioned in her 75th Anniversary speech. She said, "But, I had good teachers down here—I don't mean my own teachers in the school, I mean the people who taught me so much. Chiefly, they were the fathers and mothers of the girls. If any are living now, they are great grandfathers and great grandmothers and I am sure completely unaware of how much

their wisdom and kindness taught me. I feel very grateful to them." Edith was able to see through the foolish-
ness of some of the Baltimore attitudes to the real worth
of a great many of its people. Such reactions are always
mutual. Edith did not antagonize the Baltimore parents,
as did many of the so-called "advanced women" of that
time. Those old war horses simply despised the southern
people, who, in turn, could not abide them.

Edith had the ability to make the life of the school
interesting. "Nothing was ever dull with Miss Hamilton
around," one of my classmates wrote me. Edith thought
up the idea of having the Bryn Mawr School play
basketball with St. Timothy's, a highly successful girls'
boarding school in Catonsville, just outside of Baltimore. It was run by two sisters, Miss Polly and Miss
Sally Carter, for whom Edith had a true liking and respect. They were southern women but they had some
real educational standards and their background and
family made them acceptable and understandable to
Baltimoreans. It will be hard for anyone today to understand what a startling idea it was to suggest that those
two schools play a basketball match. The Misses Carter
told Edith it would be impossible. The newspapers
would undoubtedly write it up and the girls' names
would be in the papers. It just would not do. Edith
brought up the fact that most members of the teams
would be making their debuts in society the following
year, when the newspapers would not only give their
names but describe practically everything they were

wearing. Doubtless the Misses Carter thought that Edith, coming from the North, just could not understand what was what. And doubtless she could not.

Edith, however, was determined and suggested they get hold of the editors of the newspapers and ask them please, as a particular favor, not to write up the game. This was agreed upon and the match became a yearly event. Mrs. McIntosh, who was in the class of 1916 and subsequently became the headmistress of the Brearley School in New York, then president of Barnard College and one of the outstanding educators in the United States, said at the school's 75th Anniversary, "I think the greatest excitement that I ever had in my life was at the St. Timothy's game. Nothing could ever equal the atmosphere that surrounded this one great event of the year. We were dressed in white flannel blouses with a yellow B.M.S. and distinguished brown serge bloomers. When we acquired this blouse and these bloomers, it was really like receiving a knighthood from the Queen. We all had huge yellow chrysanthemums (St. Timothy's had white ones tied with blue bows). I never see a chrysanthemum now without having that feeling of excitement come up within me, and the feeling that the greatest of all days has come. And I'm sure that none of the wonderful athletics that you have ever had since then can possibly have the same aura of glory that particular event had for us."

I never made the team, but I felt the joyous thrill of those matches just as Mrs. McIntosh describes them, and so did all the Bryn Mawr School girls. The various other school events, such as school plays, commencement, and gymnasium contests, all were of keen interest. The school was divided into Gooks and Spooks. Why we chose those names for ourselves I have not the least remembrance, but every girl was either one or the other, and we had basketball teams and rival games which aroused great enthusiasm. What made ours of such interest and fun? Was the extraordinary vitality of mind and body of our headmistress partly responsible? I do not know, but I am sure it played a part in the great success the school achieved, an achievement against formidable odds!

Of course, the outstanding importance of the school was in its scholastic achievement. What were the educational ideas and theories of the woman who led one of the most prominent schools in the country? *Fortune* magazine, in an article describing some of our early schools, referred to Edith as an "educational comet."

In the 1959 anniversary bulletin of the Bryn Mawr School, Edith wrote of the stiff curriculum that had been required ever since the school was founded: "The idea that we might be causing inferiority complexes never occurred to me. The notion had not yet invaded school precincts and my own experience, far from leading me to it, made me convinced that the Bryn Mawr College entrance examinations could be passed by every girl who was willing to work hard, very hard in some cases, I admit.

"But it is not hard work which is dreary; it is superficial work. That is always boring in the long run, and it has always seemed strange to me that in our endless discussions about education so little stress is ever laid on the pleasure of becoming an educated person, the enormous interest it adds to life.

"The atmosphere of the school was not dull or depressing. Again and again I saw that delightful thing, an awakening to the joys of knowledge. I became convinced that real education was a matter of individual conversion."

Earlier, in an article referring to the Athenians' idea of education, she wrote:

"We need the challenge of the way the Greeks were educated. They fixed their eyes on the individual. We contemplate the millions. What we have undertaken in this matter of education has dawned upon us only lately. We are trying to do what has never been attempted before, never in the history of the world—educate all the young in a nation of over 170 millions; a magnificent idea, but we are beginning to realize what are the problems and what may be the result of mass production of education. So far, we do not seem appalled at the prospect of exactly the same kind of education being applied to all the school children from the Atlantic to the Pacific, but there is an uneasiness in the air, a realization that the individual is growing less easy to find; an idea, perhaps, of what standardization might become when the units are not machines, but human beings. . . . Our millions spend hours before television sets looking at exactly the same thing at exactly the same time. For one reason or another we are more and more ignoring differences, if not trying to obliterate them. We seem headed toward a standardization of the mind, what Goethe called 'the deadly commonplace that fetters us all.' "

Edith had no interest in theories of education and the *way* things should be taught. She by no means looked down on "educators" and "the schools for teaching teachers how to teach" that we have been developing over many years. She said to me once, "You know I am not a real educator at all." Of course she was. She was a born teacher, a great and inspired one. An old Bryn Mawr School girl said, "The Bryn Mawr School opened our eyes to the excitement of the intellectual life—we did not get it from Bryn Mawr College—but we did from the School. It was the greatest thing Miss Hamilton did." The many letters and talks I have had with girls who were at the school when Edith was headmistress all express the same thing.

It is impossible to explain just how she did it. As a personality she seemed remote, apart. The school girls were afraid of her but with pleasurable excitement. Years ago one of the girls, Grace Branhan, wrote "A Tribute," which put into words what all of us felt. She wrote:

"Miss Hamilton—even to the younger children, before we had entered the lighted circle of her classes—was a figure of high, mysterious power. When she slipped into the study hall, and took up her place at the desk, to read or mark papers, her mind remote from us and our infinitesimal concerns, the buzz and rattle of the ordinary regime sank to perfect stillness; and a hush ever followed her swift passage as she swept by us on the stairs.

"I think I do not exaggerate, or speak only for myself, when I say that she brought in with her the air of having come from some high centre of civilization, where the skies were loftier, the views more spacious, the atmosphere more free and open than with us.

"And to many of us she was the means of a higher gift than culture. Even a heedless school girl is aware, if dimly, of a noble and religious nature."

Edith always opened the school day with a brief reading, usually from the Psalms or Gospels, ending with a prayer. Mrs. McIntosh said of them:

"The spirit of those prayers made a great impression on us all as we sat in that great study hall, surrounded by the Parthenon frieze. Miss Hamilton used to stand on the platform with the light coming in through the great windows. She knew the passages from the Bible that she read to us by heart, and so she would turn her head and look out of the window as she read to us in the mornings. One passage which was her favorite, it seems to me, sums up what was really the essence of the school; it carried us through the difficult work that we had to do, and made us determined to go forward with knowledge, to take ourselves to college even when it was unpopular to go. 'Whatsoever things are good, whatsoever things are true, whatsoever things are lovely, whatsoever things are of good report, if there be any virtue, if there be any knowledge . . . think on these things.' "

Although there were more than three hundred girls in the school, Edith gave us our monthly reports individually. These interviews were held sitting on the school's back stairs. In designing the beautiful and ultramodern —for those days—school, Miss Garrett's well-known New York architect failed to provide space for offices. Mrs. McIntosh once described what every one of us girls experienced on receiving our reports when she said, "A girl went out with Miss Hamilton and sat with her on those granite stairs, where she showed us our reports, putting her hand over the report and taking it down one subject at a time. I think this in some ways rivalled in excitement the trip out to Catonsville for the St. Timothy's game. Even though she was so great and so distant in many ways, she could say just the right thing to make us want to do more or better than we were doing. When she taught us she became alive in a way that I could never describe."

Edith's talk at the 75th Anniversary was not a written speech; it was an informal talk that was taken down on a tape recorder. Part of it is revealing of Edith herself, and it gives some of her attitudes toward education.

"As I have looked back trying to think of memories to talk to you about," she said, "one thing has come to me which I had never quite realized before; how very

hard it was for me to live up to the school's sins! By that
I mean I had to take them terribly seriously, because the
only punishment ever inflicted on any of the girls was an
interview with me; and very often they were the kind of
thing you just want to laugh over. One illustration I am
going to allow myself, and the girl in question is here in
this hall. I think we would all consider her a person with
an original and adventurous turn of mind. One morning
she got up very early and went to the school house long
before anybody else was there and occupied herself in
the main study room. Many of you will remember it—
all the desks of the main school were there. During
prayers everything was as orderly as possible. But then
—prayers ended, the desk lids were raised, and out
leaped from every one a lot of very lively and very long-
legged grasshoppers! I couldn't possibly describe the
scene to you—it couldn't be described. I am sure none of
you could ever guess how long it was before the school
building was completely purified of these creatures.
Well, the terrible perpetrator of this deed was brought
down to me to be convicted of sin. And what I had to do
my best to do was not to burst out laughing. You can see
that was a duty that often was very hard on me.

"And another thing I see as very difficult; it was up
to me, even though my teachers were so good, to keep
the atmosphere of the school one where real life and
book learning were in the same world. It is so easy to get
them apart. I remember once, going into a classroom
where a small girl was beginning her recitation with

'Achilles came out of his tent on the seashore in front of a Greek camp and stood looking over the main.' It was so smooth I was suspicious. At last I said, 'and what was the main, Emma?' She answered, 'A ship blown up in the Spanish war.' I got a very clear idea of how possible it was to learn words by heart without ever thinking of their making sense."

She spoke of the high standards imposed by the close connection with Bryn Mawr College: "I can't say, though, that I myself ever thought much of college professors as educational guides for school girls. [Much laughter.] I know that is heresy, but I really think that. I fought a battle royal with the History Department of Bryn Mawr College because they wanted me to drop all history from the school. Don't send us any girls, they said, with silly stories in their heads about Alfred and the cakes, or George Washington and his little hatchet. We can teach them much better if you just leave it all to us. Well, that dreadful educational idea was defeated because the English Department at Bryn Mawr College sided with me. But all the same, I still remember with bitterness a Greek entrance examination where my girls, who had learned their Greek as Bryn Mawr College told them to, by reading Xenophon's *March of the 10,000* and the Iliad's battles of gods and men on the ringing plains of windy Troy, were asked to turn into Greek one of Aesop's fables about a frog! It was terrible and I still am angry when I think about it!

"What I prized about the close connection of the

school with the college was that it made hard work necessary. I can see myself sitting on the back stairs in the school building, telling a girl that she had failed her college entrance examination, and I can feel the heavy silence that got between us, and then I see her looking at me firmly and saying, 'Well, I've got to put off making my debut at the Bachelors' Cotillion for a year.' The Bryn Mawr School taught me that failure had its good side as well as its bad side. It did not need to create a complex; it could create courage. . . . Plato spoke for them all when he said with finality, 'Hard is the good.' " She quoted an eighth century B.C. poet: "Before the gates of Excellence the high gods have placed sweat, long is the road thereto and steep and rough at the first, but when the height is achieved then is there ease." She went on to say that "nothing effortless was among the good things the early Greeks wanted."

Does all this sound a bit grim? It was not. It is certainly as far removed as possible from the modern ideas of education to which we have become accustomed. But nothing "effortless" was among the things that Edith herself valued or found rewarding. She was able to make the idea "hard is the good" not grim, but interesting and exciting. She succeeded in presenting it as a challenge to which many of the most unlikely school girls responded.

Edith's talk continued: "A wise and witty writer has said that the spirit of American education today is 'if at first you don't succeed, try something else.' That spirit has never invaded our school." In ending her talk she said: "There is a bit of Aristotle I always like to quote. He says it is a definition of happiness. It is that, but I think it also is what education should strive for: 'the exercise of vital powers along lines of excellence, in a life affording them scope.'"

On another occasion Edith had written, "I loved teaching far and away more than anything else I did," but she did not have time to do much of it. Seeing parents, attending teachers' meetings, and the like kept her busy. She succeeded in getting in some individual teaching and tutoring at her apartment, however, or sometimes on Sunday at the school, and she taught the seniors one class in Latin. Concerning this class she wrote: "I got a great deal of fun out of teaching Virgil. I remember once translating to my class the description in the *Aeneid* of the exhausted oarsmen after the great boat race. In the next number of the school magazine there appeared: 'One whose words we always revere tells us that *Anhelitus quatit memba* should be translated, Their limbs shook from their pants.'"

Nancy de Ford Venable wrote me, "I entered Bryn Mawr School in the second grade—shy, gawky, and governess trained. I was impelled to overlook my studies and to have a good time, so I was constantly in trouble. Apparently, most of my misdemeanors were capital ones so I was frequently sent before the headmistress. In this way I became quite intimate with Miss Hamilton at a time when to the lower school she was only a distant and awe-inspiring presence. I remember a day when someone threw a spitball in class. I was innocent of the offense, but the teacher fell on me, and ordered me from the room to report to Miss Hamilton. I went down boiling with righteous indignation, secretly hoping that the teacher would draw a rebuke. Miss Hamilton listened to my diatribe with smiling tolerance, and then remarked that it was too bad that there had been injustice, 'but of course you realize, my dear Nancy, that these things never happen to the good little girls.'

"My first opportunity to enjoy the never-to-be-forgotten benefits of Miss Hamilton as a teacher came when I was in the fifth grade and she took the Latin class, which was for me pure delight. We had been put on our honor never to scribble in a translation above the text in our Virgil. One day, having mislaid my copy, I borrowed one from another girl. When I opened it in class I saw the words were written in above, and hoped that I would not be called on to translate. Miss Hamilton arrived in haste, as usual, sat down, looked around and said, 'Dear, dear, I have forgotten my book. Nancy, please lend me yours.' I rose, but would gladly have gone through the floor. She looked at the page and saw that the honor code had been broken. She finished the class and returned me the book without a comment. Nor did she ever at any time refer to the incident. I, also, held my peace, but I had a feeling that she understood."

Nancy refers to the fact that the Bryn Mawr College examinations had to be passed before a girl could graduate from the school. "The system was a cruel one as the final marks from the college only arrived two days before our commencement. I had a burning desire to graduate but seemed unable to remove my interest from basketball, where I was distinguished by my extreme incompetence, from the school paper, of which I was art editor, and from dramatics, where I had had several truly dramatic conflicts with the instructor.

"I arrived in due time before Miss Hamilton, to meet my doom, only to find that by some unimaginable good luck I had not only made the necessary points, but had passed every paper. Miss Hamilton was delighted by this unexpected reversal of all known certainties and was so kind that my face was stained with tears. She dismissed me with a smile, saying, 'We both know the Scripture, my dear Nancy. "The wicked flourish like a green bay tree." ' "

Of the Latin class and tutoring, Mrs. McIntosh has this to say: "When we reached the senior class, she taught us Latin and we read Virgil's *Aeneid* in breathless excitement. I was appointed to find her and bring her to each class. Even at the age of sixteen, I felt my heart beating as I pursued her through the school and escorted her to the classroom. She kept us absorbed through every minute of the period, exhilarated when we did well, and deeply depressed when we fell below the ideal of what we could achieve. Then one wonderful day she invited me to come once a week to her apartment to read Greek with her at sight. These visits were the crowning intellectual experience of my life."

In introducing her as a speaker at the school's 75th Anniversary celebration, Dr. John Bordley of Baltimore said:

"Her stamp and her standards will always remain with this school. When she resigned in 1922, she devoted her new freedom to thought and study, research and writing. The result of this study and this writing is now history. She no longer can be claimed as the Bryn Mawr School's Miss Hamilton, she no longer can be claimed as America's Miss Hamilton, she has become a citizen of the world." He then quoted from the citation given her in 1960 when she received an honorary degree from Yale University:

"Your retirement from the leadership of a famous preparatory school was the beginning of a new career in which you have taken the nation to school. By the sheer power of your books, you have become one of our great sources of adult education. Your scholarly love of Greek culture is no repining for a dead past, but a new dimension of depth and beauty in our civilization."

Winter at Sea Wall

⁊AFTER twenty-six years as head of the Bryn Mawr
School Edith had had enough, and she was tired out. At
the school's commencement in June, 1922, she formally
retired. The alumnae had ordered a portrait painted of
her, and in acknowledging it she said, "This only bears
out what I have been trying to teach you, and that is to
look a plain fact in the face."

In 1916, having sold their cottage in Mackinac,
Edith, Alice, Margaret, and their mother bought a place
in Hadlyme, Connecticut. When their father died in
1909, Mrs. Hamilton left Fort Wayne and came to live
in Baltimore with Edith and Margaret. She had only one
summer with them in Hadlyme, for she died the following winter. This was a great blow, as Edith was deeply
devoted to her. She was a most charming and delightful
person.

Their house at Hadlyme is old and lovely, set right
on the Connecticut River in several acres of land. Edith
loved the place but she did not like the climate in the
summer. Unlike her beloved Mackinac, it is hot and
humid. For several summers she had paid visits to my
parents in Seal Harbor, Maine, and she fell in love with

Mt. Desert Island. "The air is so stimulating," she said.
"The island is not only beautiful, it has vitality. There is
nothing tame about this ocean." So when she retired
from the school she and my mother and father, who
shared Edith's enthusiasm for Mt. Desert, bought a
summer place at Sea Wall, Mt. Desert Island, Maine.

We acquired ten acres of land on a point about a
quarter of a mile from the main road. It is a place of
spectacular beauty. Facing south is the open Atlantic
Ocean. On the east side is the Western Way and looking
north up this wide channel is a stunning view of the
mountains of Mt. Desert. We had found a house on the
main road that was for sale at an extremely low price. It
was an old house and had a very pleasing doorway, and
we thought it would be a good idea to buy it and have it
moved down to our point. It was not a good idea. The
people who made a rough calculation of what the moving would involve and cost were hopelessly off in their
estimate.

Edith had staked out just where the house was to be
placed, and it was moved in the autumn. An old woman
who had a cottage on Cranberry Island sat on her porch
watching through her binoculars as our house careened
down through the alders, over the rocks, and sometimes
into the trees. She told me later that as it got nearer and
nearer the ocean she called her husband and said, "Yesterday I thought they'd got that there house so near the
water the spray would hit it. But it keeps on comin' and
now I figure they brought it down to dump it in the

ocean."

In the summer of 1923, Edith and my family, which included my nephew, Dorian Reid, aged five, and I, all went to Sea Wall where we spent a glorious summer. The previous autumn we had worked out with our contractor certain alterations to the house which were to be completed by the following June and which included the addition of three bathrooms. When we arrived for the summer all the fixtures for the three were installed and in place but there was not a wall around any of them. It was a ludicrous sight, causing much merriment. My father commented, "Open bathrooms, openly arrived at." However, we got some wallboard and sealed up one of them before nightfall.

Both my father and I were fond of carpentering and we put up partitions, made endless bookshelves, and at Edith's suggestion paneled the whole sitting room in cypress wood. I was very proud of our achievement until once I overheard my mother and Edith in conversation, the gist of which was that the more they saw of hand carpentering the better they liked the machine product!

Edith loved to lie on the rocks and bathe in the pools left by the tide as it went out; the open ocean is far too cold for swimming. She took long walks and climbed many of the mountains. She often said that there were few walks—often scrambles—as beautiful as the mountain paths on Mt. Desert Island. She read many detective stories and told us practically every day of the week that she would never again as long as she lived do anything of consequence.

Edith read aloud better than anyone I have known and we spent many pleasant evenings listening to her read from the works of P. G. Wodehouse, whom we all found most entertaining. There was, of course, much conversation. My father was professor of geological-physics at the Johns Hopkins University but he also had a fluent knowledge of Latin, the Bible, and literature generally. My mother had recently completed her play about Florence Nightingale (published by Macmillan in 1922). The conversations covered almost every subject that exists.

As the autumn approached Edith and I decided that we, with Dorian, would spend the winter at Sea Wall. To say that the house was not winterized would be an understatement of major proportions. Edith often asked me why I bothered to shut the windows, as the wind blew right through the walls. It also swept under the house and up through the floor, making the rugs jump up and down.

Our water supply came from a well, and the pipe to the house had been dug down four feet so that it would not freeze, but then it came up and under the house and what were we going to do about that? The local plumber said there was nothing that could be done and it would be impossible for us to stay in that house through the winter. My father, however, wrapped some cakes of paraffin around the pipes and said confidently that they would not freeze, and they did not, to the astonishment of all the natives of Sea Wall.

My mother and father left for Baltimore shortly after the middle of September, leaving us to a most brilliant and colorful autumn. Edith, who by then had acquired a great enthusiasm for the place, declared that the ocean was bluer than elsewhere! That there never was goldenrod so golden and that the trees that turned scarlet were redder and more striking than autumn foliage elsewhere! As for the air, she said it had a quality of exhilaration beyond her powers of description. She was starting to head up the group of people known as Maniacs, who consider Maine superior to all other localities! She would clap her hands and say, "Isn't this a *joy*." All her life she had a passionate love for the out of doors. The beauties of quiet, peaceful scenery did not appeal to her much. She loved the mountains and ocean but, for her, the hand of man must not intrude. She once wrote in dismay of an inn in Zermatt, "the window boxes were so flourishing that one was perpetually looking at the Matterhorn through a wreath of pink geraniums." The open ocean, however, she loved most of all. Once when a storm was brewing and the waves were dashing against our rocks sending the spray high into the air, Edith said, "This is the ocean as I love it best, in magnificent protest against its boundaries." There was nothing "tame" about our scenery.

As the winter closed in our open fireplaces were hopelessly inadequate to keep us warm and we bought an iron stove which burned coal and never let it go out. We found an energetic local woman who engaged to come down each day and get us a midday meal. Edith got the suppers and, as she was always a gifted cook, those suppers were very good indeed. A road had been made from the so-called highway down to the house. It was a road, that is, if one's idea of a road is elastic enough—no car could possibly go up or down it during the winter snows and rains. The grocer would leave our supplies on the main road and Edith would walk up with Dorian's sled and fetch them down. She loved these walks, which she usually took alone, and she would come back looking radiant. "It is just *rapturous* out there," she would often exclaim.

Dorian would be six years old in the middle of November and early in October Edith took me aside and said, "You know, Doris, the boy can't *read!*" Her face registered as much astonishment as if he were about to be six*teen!* Although she had never taught small children she said she would undertake to teach him to read and write and suggested that I tackle the arithmetic. We decided that twenty minutes twice a day would be adequate for lessons. It was. By spring Dorian could read and write, add and subtract. Decades later Edith would laugh over the endless discussions and "to-dos" educators were making over how and when reading, writing, and arithmetic should be taught. She said she believed in Plato's theories: he wrote that the most important part of education was in the nursery when the children were very young. They must first of all learn the alphabet in order to learn to read, but this presented no difficulty because, after all, he said, there were not many letters in the alphabet. For arithmetic, he suggested that the Egyptian method should be adopted; they made up arithmetical games with apples. Edith said she was quite sure that Plato said red apples, but she could not vouch for this! Whatever method Edith adopted, it certainly succeeded with Dorian, and when we went to New York he was so far ahead for his age that he had to go into a class with older children. This was very much frowned upon by "educators" at that time. Edith thought they had a point, but felt that to hold a child back deliberately would result in his getting bored with his studies, which in her opinion was the worst thing that could happen. To Edith, the great, if not the greatest, advantage of becoming an educated person was "the enormous interest it adds to life."

In the course of the winter she told and read Dorian stories from the Bible. She always felt that the Bible was the great book of human experience, and that the King James version contained some of the most beautiful prose in the English language. Leaving aside all religious connotations, she said, many times, "It permeates our great literature and our great art, much of which would be incomprehensible without a knowledge of the Bible." Edith did not think that five years was a bit too soon to start acquiring this knowledge, but she felt that reading some of the Bible stories to Dorian would present diffi-

culties. Dorian had an inquiring mind. The previous
summer he and Edith were sitting on the rocks by the
ocean and he asked her if God had "made all this," to
which she answered, "Yes." He then said that his grandfather had told him that when, millions of years ago, this
world came into being there was no person on it. "Who
saw God make it?" he exploded. "You can't be sure,
Eda, you can't be sure." Edith wondered with amused
uneasiness what questions he would ask her about the
story of Adam and Eve, for instance. She got around the
problem by omitting to read that story!

Edith had a great love of animals and regardless of
where she was living, in a New York apartment or at Sea
Wall, she always had a cat or a dog, usually one of each.
During the winter at Sea Wall she acquired a six-week-
old Newfoundland puppy, a wire-haired fox terrier, and
I cannot remember how many cats. They all attended
the Christmas party we gave for Dorian and the local
children who were his playmates.

Many of the winter days were most beautiful.
Huge cakes of ice, some as big as our house, floated in
the ocean. Green and blue and sometimes greenish blue
colors radiated from them as the light and sun shifted. As
the tide went out the salt water froze white on the rocks
and looked like snow. When the temperature suddenly
dropped and the water became warmer than the air, the
ocean steamed, Edith said, like a supernatural, giant tea-
kettle. "It looks positively wicked," she often exclaimed.
She also loved the quiet starlit nights when the ground

was covered with snow and "the stars seemed incredibly near." The beauty of the outdoors meant more to Edith than just pleasure and enjoyment. It went far deeper than that; it gave her a spiritual elevation as did great art, great poetry, and great thought.

As the winter wore on, it was clear that Edith's health and vitality were rapidly returning and that spark in her eye which was so characteristic of her all her life was coming back. During that time she was obviously thinking a great deal, but about what she never spoke. In March she was getting restless and said she wanted to "get back into life." We went to Baltimore and stayed with my parents until June, when we all returned to Sea Wall for the summer.

She spent practically every summer there for the next forty years. Edith celebrated her ninety-fifth birthday in August 1962 by her beloved rocks and ocean. She loved the place more than any other spot on earth. In 1960 she wrote her family from Sea Wall, "It has been a summer of bad weather and really cold, but I so love it up here that rain and fog are nicer here than good weather elsewhere, and today the fog has cleared and I see a blue ocean which sparkles—what Aeschylus calls 'The never numbered laughter of sea waves.' They do seem to be laughing."

The last words she wrote to a friend, shortly before her death, were, "I do so want to get to Sea Wall. All my vague miseries I feel will be dispersed by the sea winds."

A New Career—New York

⤷IN THE AUTUMN of 1924, Edith, Dorian, and I settled in New York. Before the winter in Sea Wall, and for several winters previously, I had left Baltimore and gone to New York to live in order to continue my studies in music. Edith did not want to go back to Baltimore.

Apart from her one class in Virgil at the Bryn Mawr School and the tutoring she managed to get, her life as headmistress had been a trial to her. The school had been such a great success that it is difficult to believe how thankful she was to be rid of it. But she was, and Baltimore had little attraction for her. Furthermore, my mother took a very dim view of my living alone in New York, and suggested that Edith spend the winter with me. Edith did not particularly care where she spent the winter, nor was she thinking of what she might do next. She was essentially a scholar, a student, a voracious reader, and she looked forward with joy to her anticipated leisure. A friend wrote me that "once when I had dropped in to see Edith, she exclaimed delightedly, 'I have been in *such* good company today.' Upon my enquiring rather enviously who these delightful visitors had been, her answer was 'Plato.' " She joined me in an apartment and there, it turned out, we lived together for many years, going with my parents and various friends to Sea Wall in the summers.

During our first year I taught music and Edith kept house, looked after Dorian, and, of course, read, studied, and thought. Her battered and scribbled-up volume of the Greek tragedies was always by her bed. For decades her absorption and joy had been to read, in the original text, the Greek tragedians; she had no interest in translations. She made notes and marks on the margins of her volume for her own reference, which were usually incomprehensible to anyone else. Equally well-worn volumes of the great writers of that ancient period were also her daily companions. Plato, Homer, Thucydides, Herodotus, and the rest she had studied and absorbed and loved since her early youth. She had little or no interest in books *about* Greece. I am sure that the idea of doing anything in particular with her unusual knowledge of Greek literature and thought did not occur to her. What made her start on a new, and what turned out to be her essential, career? What made her start writing? The story is revealing.

One afternoon a small group of intimate friends were sitting around the tea table at number 24 Gramercy Park in New York and one of them said, "Edith, tell us something about the Greek tragedies. I really don't know the difference between Aeschylus, Sophocles, and Euripides." "*My dear child!*" Edith exclaimed, and she jumped up, got down her volume of the Greek plays, and translated bits from each of the poets. She then started talking about and explaining Aeschylus, the tragedian for whom she cared most. Suddenly she said rather wistfully, "Oh, I am so afraid you don't like Aeschylus." There was a burst of laughter, and one of us said, "She talks about Aeschylus exactly as though he were her eldest son!" Another remarked, "She made me feel she must just have had lunch with him!"

From then on our little group met regularly to prod Edith with questions on almost every subject conceivable. After one discussion concerning the idea of tragedy, Rosamond Gilder, then an editor of *Theatre Arts Monthly* and one of our group, said that Edith must write it all down and send it in to the magazine. Edith said she had never written for publication and did not think that she could. Much urging and beseeching ensued. Finally, truly disturbed, Edith said, "*Please* do not press me so. How would you feel if I were imploring you to attempt to become an opera singer?" But the pressure continued and finally, after some weeks, the article was written and Edith's important and unique talent was instantly recognized. Mrs. Edith J. R. Isaacs, founder and editor-in-chief of *Theatre Arts Monthly* published with enthusiasm the article on tragedy. She said to Edith, "You know, Miss Hamilton, you are a poet." Edith laughed when she told me this. But Mrs. Isaacs was a great help and encouragement to Edith.

When our group at Gramercy Park would praise

something Edith had written, she would smile and say, "Oh *dear* Rosamond" or "*Dear* Johnnie." To her, such praise was just an expression of friendship. I said to her once, "Well, you can't say 'Dear Mrs. Isaacs,' because she hardly knows you." When Edith delivered her essay on comedy and started talking in her usual vivid fashion, Mrs. Isaacs listened with interest and then said: "If that is what you want to say, go home and write it down and include it in your article. You are that unusual combination, a gifted talker and a gifted writer. To be a gifted talker can be fatal to a writer."

After several of her articles on the Greek playwrights had appeared in *Theatre Arts Monthly,* Elling Aannestad, an editor of W. W. Norton & Company, "spotted a real writer" and asked her to do a book for them on Greece. She immediately said she would not and could not. She told him to go to the public library where he would find file drawer after file drawer listing books on Greece. What could she possibly say that had not already been said? She then told him what folly it would be for his firm to publish a book on Greece by an unknown writer, in no way recognized as a Greek scholar, and not even a professor in a university. She mustered her arguments and with her usual intensity threw herself into an attempt to dissuade him from trying to get her to write a book. But he persisted. He brought her a contract. She refused to sign it, saying it would be unfair to him to commit his firm to publish what she might write. But he persisted. In the end he won. The book was written and *The Greek Way* was published in 1930. It received instant acclaim and its popularity grew steadily. In the 1940's it was published in a paperback edition and by now it is considered a classic.

Not long ago someone asked Edith what made her start writing. "I was bullied into it," she answered truthfully.

As the years went on and her books and articles continued to appear, people have asked me such questions as: Where did she write? How long did she write each day? Did she dictate or write in longhand? Once, a reporter who was about to interview her said to me, "I think I can just see her sitting upright at her desk producing a manuscript as neat as she herself looks." What this young man thought he could see was about as far from reality as anything could possibly be. Edith always wrote sitting in an armchair with a pad, or any bit of paper she could lay her hands on, in her lap. She frequently used the backs of envelopes. She scratched out, rewrote over passages only partially rubbed out, put inserts in the margins. The result was something next to illegible. The idea of copying it over so that a secretary could read it bored Edith almost beyond endurance.

She was very fond of cooking and occasionally wrote down recipes. These were also put on bits of paper or old envelopes, and this caused some difficulties. When she sent her translation of one of the Greek plays to her publisher, an agitated secretary called me up and said that there was something she could not understand.

Right after the first chorus was a paragraph headed
"Onion Soup for Four."

To these little idiosyncracies was added a further
complication. Her kindliness and sense of responsibility
often led her to employ secretaries so inept that she
feared, and rightly, that no one else would possibly give
them a job.

Her range of interest was wide and varied. An idea
would come to her and she would jot it down on whatever lay nearest at hand. The last page of her address
book reads as follows:

Mrs. J. G. Wallace
Quincy St.
Alexandria.

                    Chippers National Biscuit Co.
                              Nabisco.
From bondage to spiritual faith, from faith to courage, from
courage to liberty, from liberty to abundance, from abundance
to selfishness, from selfishness to complacency. From complacency to apathy, and apathy to despondency. From despondency back to bondage, with faith and liberty to be won again.
              (Boiled linseed oil)

How did this method of writing fit in with her published works, which were noted for their finish and clarity, or, as one critic commented, "her finely chiseled
prose"? I think the explanation was that she felt it of no
importance or interest how she wrote, or where, or on
what. She threw her whole mind and heart into an effort
to put into words what she profoundly believed. She
never "tossed off" anything.

She had a power of concentration beyond that of anyone I have known. Most authors, scientists, people doing original work inevitably require a certain number of specified, uninterrupted hours for their project. It takes a bit of time just to settle down and get started. Not so Edith! Hundreds of times I heard her say, after chatting idly with the family, "Dinner will not be ready for fifteen minutes. I think I will do some work." She would get up, turn off her hearing aid, and go to her chair beside the window, and before she had even sat down it was clear that her mind was completely concentrated and the whole outside world blotted out. Her one and only physical disability, being hard of hearing, had an occasional advantage. She could tune out.

Once a friend dropped in to see us and asked Edith idly what she had been doing that morning. "Oh," said Edith, "I was going downtown in the subway and I finally got that line in the *Agamemnon* translated into the original meter." One can see her in the midst of that bedlam peculiar to the subway probably tapping out the rhythm with her foot, her mind so concentrated that the mad confusion surrounding her was nonexistent.

Maine was another world from that of New York, but it, too, had its distractions. One summer we acquired a sailboat and, with an assortment of nieces and nephews who were always there, Edith and I—we never had a man along—and two or three children would frequently go off for several days' cruise. Edith often said that the compliment she had received in her long life that pleased her most was when one of the little boys, aged nine, said, "You know, I would just as soon have Eda along as not." She did all the cooking, but often on a rocky beach, after the meal was over, she would move a few feet away from the general pandemonium that only small children can produce, pull a pencil out of her pocket, and settle down to write. When it seemed time to go, she tucked her pencil and paper away, but at home she could start again wherever she had left off. It seemed that she carried her detachment and absorption around with her and could drop into her inner sanctum at any moment she chose.

Another time in Maine, Edith was sitting on our porch, obviously concentrating, when one of the older children sauntered up. No one ever thought of not interrupting her.

"Edith," he said, "have you got a good detective story?"

"*The Body in the Library* is good."

"Oh, there is always a corpse in the library in books."

Edith started laughing. "You can't get a corpse into a book."

A smile spread over his young face. "You win, Edith! Come on down to the rocks. The tide is thundering in."

"No, I'm going to do some work. I think I have an idea."

"I'll bet it is a good one," the boy said laughingly as

he strolled off. He had hardly turned his back when that look of complete absorption came over Edith's face. She reached for a pencil and started writing on the edge of the Sunday newspaper.

One afternoon our children broke into the pump house, having apparently an uncontrollable desire to find out how the pump worked. They succeeded in breaking a pipe, thereby making the most incredible mess. Edith and my father spent an hour or more mopping up and putting things to rights. That evening Edith remarked how fortunate she was to have so full a life. My father burst out laughing and said, "That your life is fortunate is open to question. But that it is full, there is no doubt whatever!"

As the years rolled on, our children grew up and married. Then came the next generation. They, of course, had their own parents to look after them, which made the situation quite different. But they in turn spent their summers at Sea Wall and they loved it as their parents did and do. Sea Wall has meant so much to so many people.

Edith became good friends with many of the Maine folk. They were truly unusual and distinctive people. Most of the men and their forebears had lived on the water—the women never went near it. The men were strong, self-reliant, taciturn, and extremely kind. They would instinctively go to the aid of anyone who seemed to need it, particularly on the water. In the early days, before I learned to cope with Maine coast weather, I would unexpectedly get caught out on the ocean in a blanket of fog. Often George Dolliver, a lobster fisherman, seemed to appear out of nowhere and steer me to land.

Once I was out in the boat with several of the children, and as night came on a dense fog suddenly descended upon us. Edith, who saw the situation from the house, ran up to Mr. Dolliver's and told him where she thought we must be. He had just sat down to his evening meal but, without saying a word, he got up and pulled on his boots. Edith told me she said to him, "I can't have you go before you have eaten your dinner and those delicious hot biscuits that Mrs. Dolliver has made." He smiled and said, "Don't say another word, Miss Hamilton," and took himself off to his lobster boat and went after us.

Amos Dolliver, George Dolliver's father, told us to moor our boat by the small dock he had made for himself in a cove below his house. This was most convenient, as it was impossible for us to keep the boat in the open ocean in front of our place, but pulling up our tender above the tide was quite an effort. Once when we went down to the dock, we found some well-cut, bark-stripped logs laid out over the rocks. We stopped in to see Mr. Dolliver, and Edith said, "Those logs are the greatest possible help. You must let us pay for them."

"I reckon as I can drag my own skiff over them logs."

"But you haven't got a skiff."

"How do you know I won't get one?"

Edith seemed to be losing the argument and said, "Now, Mr. Dolliver, we use your dock, we drive over your land almost every day." Mr. Dolliver interrupted, "Stop right there, Miss Hamilton. All this land belongs to God. He lets me use it and I want you to use it."

Edith often called on Amos Dolliver, who was an old man then, and she told me many times of the truly intelligent and wise observations he made.

Then there was Mrs. Harper, who taught in the little public schoolhouse nearby. When Edith took her usual long walks, she would often drop in to see her. Mrs. Harper told me once how much Edith's visits meant to her. There were, of course, other State of Mainers who became to us an integral part of Sea Wall, but they remained Mr. and Mrs. There were no first names. The next generation, who were the age of our children and who are now in their forties, do not seem to have the rugged self-reliance that was so evident in their fathers and grandfathers. When I would comment on this, Edith would say that for centuries every generation thought that the next generation was probably going to the dogs, and the attitude bored her. Nonetheless she agreed with me that whether or not this younger generation was better or worse than their parents, they were certainly different.

Owing to certain family developments, the Reid children came to live permanently with Edith and me in New York. She did not think of herself as "deciding" to take them on. In the circumstances it seemed best for them to leave Baltimore and come to us. Here they were. In her mind that was all there was to it.

Few women are able to lead a normal, full domestic life and at the same time achieve an outstandingly successful professional career. A friend said to me, shortly after Edith retired from the Bryn Mawr School in 1922, that she should become a professor of Greek in a university, and that that was the life she was made for. He was wrong. She was so made that it would have been impossible for her to make study and writing the main object of her life.

Her ability to concentrate at any moment, to catch ten minutes here and an hour or so there, explains how, living the life she did, she was still able to write seven books and a number of essays and book reviews, and in the latter part of her life—that is, after she was eighty—start making public addresses. She always ran a large household. When Dorian went to boarding school, his two younger sisters came to live with us. Once their younger brother, aged thirteen, who had been fired out of every school he had ever been sent to, arrived on our doorstep and spent the winter with us.

In the autumn of 1929 I went into the investment counsel house of Loomis, Sayles & Company, where I stayed for twenty-nine years. I was at the office all day long, including a half day Saturday. I have often heard people speak in praise of women who can hold down full-time jobs. They are wrong, quite wrong. I have some-

times thought that a professional job was a rest cure
compared to the never-ending demands of family life.

Why did Edith undertake so much? In the first
place, it was some years before she took her writing seriously. When her *Three Greek Plays* came out in 1937
and one critic referred to her as "our leading classicist,"
she burst out laughing and said, "How ridiculous." In
the second place, Edith's work was never as important to
her as the people who surrounded her. I remember once
she asked me to look over an income tax form she had
just made out, to be sure it was correct. "Well," I said,
"you are enclosing the publisher's statement of your
royalties but you do not include that amount under 'income.'" "Oh," she said with a wave of her hand, "I
don't count my royalties." I continued, "You wrote the
books, didn't you! And under the heading 'occupation'
you write 'none.'"

In the spring of 1929 we decided to take a trip
abroad. Edith had finished *The Greek Way*, which was
in the hands of her publishers. She had traveled a good
deal in her lifetime in England, Europe, China, and
Japan but, surprisingly, she had never been to Greece.

We wanted to avoid the much-publicized terrific
heat of the summers there, and we arrived on March 19.
If we had gone for winter sports, we could hardly have
done better. I have rarely been so cold. As for the glories
of the Grecian wildflowers, no wildflower would have
raised its head in that temperature. Be all this as it may,
Edith, Dorian—aged eleven—and I had a wonderful trip

in that indescribable land. No photographs, however excellent, can convey the Acropolis and no words can
truly describe it. Delphi, Corinth, Sunion, and the rest
have to be seen to be believed. As soon as we reached
Athens we went up on the Acropolis. Edith sat for a
long time on the steps of the Parthenon, but what was
going through her mind and heart I did not know.

There were few planes at that time, and we went and
returned by boat. This was no hardship, as Edith always
loved a long ocean voyage, and for Dorian the trip was
grand fun. Edith was a delightful traveling companion.
She enjoyed everything, and her ability to recount with
great vividness stories of the past was a joy. Once when
we were in Greece, she turned to Dorian and quoted:
"The mountains look on Marathon—And Marathon
looks on the sea." Then, with her exceptional ability to
develop a thrilling tale, she told of the Greek victory over
the hordes of Persians and ended the Byron quotation:

> A king sat on the rocky brow
> Which looks o'er sea born Salamis;
> And ships, by thousands, lay below,
> And men and nations all were his.
> He counted them at break of day—
> And when the sun set, where were they?

Dorian turned with shining eyes, looked over the
Aegean Sea and exploded, "None of them has come
back yet, Eda!" I confess, such was the excitement that
Edith got into her storytelling that my reaction was
about the same as Dorian's.

After about two weeks in Greece we picked up a cruise ship which took us to Cairo, where we stayed for a week. Each day we rode on camels out into the desert. Of the pyramids Edith wrote later on: "They look to be nothing made by hands but part of the basic structure of the earth. Where the wind lifts the sand into shapes of gigantic geometry—triangles which, as one watches, pass into curves and break again into sharp-pointed outlines, a cycle of endless change as fixed as the movement of the stars against the immensity of the desert which never changes—the pyramids, immutable, immovable, are the spirit of the desert incased in granite."

Our trip was a delight from start to finish, and fortunately we did not know how many years would pass before we got off again.

Her years in New York were interesting and rewarding. The fact that she was no longer a headmistress was enormously freeing. An old friend of ours wrote to me: "The minute Edith retired from the school she came out from her remoteness to become warmly accessible as a personality. Such is her agelessness that anyone, young or old, who knows her soon thinks of her as Edith, and calls her just that."

Our group in New York was joined by John Mason Brown and Dorna McCollester, both of whom were editors of *Theatre Arts Monthly*, Donald Oenslager, Elling Aannestad, and Dorothy Sands. The writers in the group would read what they had written or were working on. Once when Edith was struggling over her chapter on Cicero for her second book, *The Roman Way*, she sent a note to John Brown: "Doris says you thought you would come down tomorrow and hear a bit of Cicero—but alas, I have not got the M.S. It is being typed. I assure you—oh so fervently—it is your gain. I suspect the gentleman is dull. I know I am. Ever yours, dear boy, E. H."

Sometimes we would play games. The book *Ask Me Another* had just come out and a question read to Edith was, "How many men are there in a U.S. regiment?" She said that was the kind of information that never stuck in her mind, and added, "Why, you know I would do well if I could remember how many soldiers were in a Roman Legion."

One could hardly mention a poem that she did not know by heart. She recited the whole of "Horatius at the Bridge" to Dorian. Her memory was not confined to poetry. I have often heard her quote paragraphs of prose. Dorna McCollester once said to me, "When Edith talked of some distinguished figure in the past, she did not tell me what he thought, she quoted exactly what he said."

This unusual memory did not include names or faces; she could never remember either. Once her publisher, Warder Norton, gave a dinner for her, to meet Harry Overstreet. She sailed into the room, held out her hand, and said, "Oh, Mr. Overbeck, this is indeed a pleasure." Realizing, from his expression, that she had got the name wrong, she turned to Warder and said, "As Mr. Overton has told me." Warder wrote on a scrap of paper, which he passed on to me, "Please take Edith home before she calls him overshoes." I gave this to Edith. She burst out laughing and handed it to Mr. Overstreet. The evening was made.

Her second book, *The Roman Way*, published in 1932, was received with critical acclaim; her *Prophets of Israel* was published in 1936. The following year *Three Greek Plays* came out, which was her translation of the *Prometheus Bound*, the *Agamemnon*, and *The Trojan Women*, with introductions. I believe she had been working on these translations off and on over a period of years. In 1942 *The Greek Way* was republished, with five additional chapters which included studies of Pindar, Herodotus, Thucydides, and Homer.

In 1939 Raymond Everitt, vice-president of Little, Brown & Company, decided that Bulfinch had become dated and that a new, comprehensive mythology was a sound publishing project. He talked this idea over with his friend John Mason Brown, who suggested that he discuss the proposition with Edith. Mr. Everitt called to see her and immediately aroused her interest. At the end of the interview he asked if she would write a brief outline of a possible mythology, giving perhaps some chapter headings. Edith said at once that she would not think of doing that. "Mr. Everitt," she continued, "writing on any subject is to me a voyage of discovery. I have never composed an outline for any of my books. This is one of my weaknesses, but there you have it. To write an all-inclusive mythology would interest me enormously, but just how I developed it would depend on what a restudy of the vast numbers of mythological tales suggested." Apparently Mr. Everitt was willing to take a chance, for he sent her a contract for the book, which she signed. Edith spent three years working on this book. It was, indeed, an exhaustive task, and was published in 1942. In her Foreword she writes: "A book on Mythology must draw from widely different sources. Twelve hundred years separate the first writers through whom the myths have come down to us, from the last, and there are stories as unlike each other as *Cinderella* and *King Lear*. To bring them all together in one volume is really somewhat comparable to doing the same for the stories of English literature from Chaucer to the ballads, through Shakespeare and Marlowe . . . and so on, ending with, say, Tennyson and Browning. . . .

"Faced with this problem, I determined at the outset to dismiss any idea of unifying the tales. That would have meant either writing *King Lear,* so to speak, down to the level of *Cinderella*—the vice versa procedure being obviously not possible—or else telling in my own way stories which were in no sense mine and had been told by great writers in ways they thought suited their subjects. I do not mean, of course, that a great writer's style can be reproduced. . . . My aim has been nothing more ambitious than to keep distinct for the reader the very different writers from whom our knowledge of the myths comes. For example, Hesiod is a notably simple writer and devout; he is naïve, even childish, sometimes crude, always full of piety. Many of the stories in this book are told only by him. Side by side with them are stories told only by Ovid, subtle, polished, artificial, self-conscious, and the complete skeptic. My effort has been to make the reader see some difference between writers who were so different. After all, when one takes up a book like this, one does not ask how entertainingly the author has retold the stories, but how close he has brought the reader to the original."

Edith never wrote anything for publication that was not accepted. Everything to which she turned her hand was a success. The Bryn Mawr School was outstanding; her career as an author and classical scholar needs no comment; her speeches were exceptional. But the adjectives happy, contented, or self-satisfied would never come to mind when one thinks of Edith.

I believe this was true of her all her life, more on account of the things she did not say than the things which she did say. She would read a favorable review of one of her books with civilized pleasure but it was evident that her satisfaction did not go deep. If she read a sentence which seemed to her extravagant praise, she would laughingly say of the reviewer, "He's a goose." If she happened to know the reviewer she would say, "He is a dear goose." When John Mason Brown wrote of her, "In any period Edith Hamilton would be exceptional; in ours she is unique," she put down the article, and exclaimed, "Oh that *darling* boy!"

Her periods of "deep depression" I never knew at the time. Decades later when I was talking about our winter at Sea Wall she astonished me by saying, "That was a hard winter for me. I had been a very busy headmistress and suddenly I had nothing to do. As you well know I never thought of writing and I somehow had a wretched feeling of futility."

Anyone of her intensity, and there are few, is bound to have strong reactions. There is a sentence in her chapter on tragedy: "We differ in nothing more than in our power to feel." She was the possessor of that power.

One evening after dinner a group of us were sitting around and Edith was speculating gaily about what was going to happen to one of our acquaintances when he reached the Pearly Gates. Someone said, "Well, I *know* what is going to happen when Edith confronts St. Peter. Her head will be bowed and she will say, '*Mea culpa, mea culpa, mea maxima culpa.* Father, I am not fit to enter the Kingdom of Heaven.' St. Peter will put his arm around her and say, 'My dear child, the Kingdom of Heaven wants you.' She will go through the gate, her head still bowed. Suddenly she will spy St. Augustine. She will remember that he said that little children who had not been baptized would go to purgatory. Her head will fly up. Her eyes will blaze. She will point her finger at him and say, 'What are *you* doing here?' "

Rosamond Gilder; her sister, Francesca Gilder Palmer, and her husband, Dr. Walter Palmer, and their children; Dorna McCollester and her husband, Parker

McCollester, and their children; as well as Edith, Dorian, and I all lived for many years at 24 Gramercy Park. We would frequently have dinner parties at one apartment or the other. Edith was always the center. "Nothing was ever *dull* when she was around," as one of her former Bryn Mawr School pupils said. But she did not like to sit talking indefinitely. When she had had enough, it seemed she would vanish. We would look up and she just was not there. This was always referred to as "Edith's disappearing act" and we never figured out quite how she did it!

Edith was devoted to Dr. Palmer, who was the distinguished head of the Columbia Medical Center. She enjoyed the jokes he loved to tell, and once when he wrote her a limerick of questionable propriety, she composed the following reply:

> A doctor once highly respected
> Whose failing nobody suspected
> Gave himself quite away
> So that I with dismay
> A depraved sense of humor detected.

During the course of those years she saw a good deal of the Palmer and McCollester children, and she would sometimes repeat verses and jingles to them. "I do wonder why all this nonsense sticks in my memory," she often said.

In addition to the inhabitants of 24 Gramercy Park, Edith made many friends in New York, chiefly of my generation. But, as everyone who knew her said, "Edith is ageless." Their enthusiasm for her writing was a major support and encouragement to her. Then Dorian and his sister Betsy went to college, and although they spent the holidays and summers with us, the winter household was reduced to their younger sister, Mary, who was by then in her teens.

The Christmas and Easter holidays were always animated. I remember with particular vividness Dorian's first Easter holiday from college. He had never quite recovered from Edith's early tutoring and he entered Amherst at the age of sixteen. He had written us with starry-eyed and typical undergraduate zeal that he had joined the Young Communist League. He wrote several times that a number of his group would be in New York for the holidays and we gathered that he wanted to be sure that we would receive them with proper respect.

Edith asked me if I thought that we should serve the comrades cocktails and highballs. She said that a number of parents with whom she had talked served liquor to their college boys, feeling it better for them to drink at home than to go chasing around New York City. We both finally agreed that we would not pay untold sums for alcohol and we would take a chance on their staying at home.

Dorian arrived one afternoon and that evening the comrades trickled in. Many college freshmen are untidy but those boys looked as if they had just come out of a mud hole. There was one young girl among them whom Edith always referred to as the "lady comrade." Her hat, which she wore on one ear, fascinated Edith because, defying all the laws of gravity, it stayed there.

There was one young Englishman, an exchange student from Cambridge, who appeared to think that no American had any education at all. He liked to talk to Edith and was astonished that she seemed to know something about ancient Greece.

I decided that the boys had not had a bath since they had been to college because they now showed such a passion for them. Edith said to me, "You know I can never get into the bathroom as there is always a comrade in the tub. Also, their ideas about 'sharing' apply to bath towels." We finally hid ours in a bureau drawer.

Day after day and night after night and into the small hours of the morning they sat around talking about how they were going to reform the world and get rid of the outrageous capitalistic system. Toward the end of the holiday I, who had feared that they might spend most of the time "on the town," found myself saying, "Why don't you fellows go out and see this city? There is a good movie," and so on. The climax came when the English boy came down with German measles and I caught it from him. Edith always maintained that I had been a confirmed capitalist ever since.

Edith spent more and more time on her writing, but her way of life did not change much. She always went to Hadlyme, usually in the spring and autumn, to be with her sisters. They would come to New York during the winter to visit her, and they came to Sea Wall for a while each summer. She continued to "keep house," with all the endless detail it involves, and she saw innumerable people with whom she had made close connections. Her writing absorbed her increasingly, but, as always, the people who mattered to her came first.

Then in the spring of 1943 my firm asked me to move to Washington and take over their office in that city. My friends did not like the thought of my leaving New York, but the reaction to Edith's going, too, caused —it is no exaggeration to say—a riot. I was reminded that Edith was nearly seventy-seven years old and could not have so many years ahead of her; that it was practically impossible to find a place to live in Washington (it was wartime) and if we found one, it was a hopeless city in which to live. I must not let her go. "What will we do without her?" This and much more was dinned into my distressed ears.

I cannot overstate how little I wanted to go. I had lived in New York for some twenty-five years and it was home to me. On the other hand, it was clear that I should not turn down such an opportunity and that, characteristically, was what concerned Edith. Furthermore, where she lived made less difference to her than it does to most people.

I complained to an old friend of mine, "You know, I don't know a *soul* in Washington." She said, "Well, you are going with Edith, and after a few months you will find she has collected around her the most interesting people in that city."

In June of 1943 we packed up and moved to Washington, and there we lived for the next twenty years.

Washington, D.C.

⟶SHORTLY after we reached Washington we bought a small house at 2448 Massachusetts Avenue, the back of which faced Rock Creek Park. Looking out of our windows one would not suppose there was a house within miles of us. We had a small garden which we filled with azaleas, and in the front, on Massachusetts Avenue, was a particularly lovely cherry tree. Edith of course had her dog and her cat.

There were vicissitudes. In the spring of 1944 Edith broke her hip. At the same time my father, who was eighty-five years old, became critically ill. While Edith was on crutches, she got herself over to Baltimore and was at his bedside when he died.

After my father's death in June, my mother came to live with us in Washington. She realized that she could not live alone in the big Baltimore house and she told me that she wanted it sold as quickly as possible. Her forebears were Baltimoreans for generations back. She and my father had lived in that house for about sixty years, but she was a gay and gallant soul and it was hard to keep in mind what a wrench such a drastic change must have been for her.

The doctor told me that Edith's hip had mended completely but that she would probably always need crutches. He said that older people usually did not know what made them fall and, in order to avoid doing the same thing again, they would naturally hang on to their canes or crutches. I told him to say all this to Edith; there was no point in saying it to me. He did so. Edith laid aside her crutches and never picked them up again.

Edith had started writing her book on the Gospels, *Witness to the Truth*. Shortly before we left New York she had given three lectures at the house of a friend on Socrates, St. Paul and Christ. As was her invariable custom, she had spent considerable time preparing these talks and I thought that doubtless the spadework for her book on the Gospels had been largely completed. I could not have been more mistaken. Edith spent almost four years on *Witness to the Truth*. Without the encouragement of her friend Elling Aannestad I doubt if this book would ever have been finished. Questions kept coming to her mind which inhibited her. Should she undertake a subject of such profound importance? Had she or had she not got across her points? (She never doubted the validity of her points.) Was what she wrote of any interest? Once she rewrote one of her chapters and read it aloud to Elling. He said idly, "It is longer than your first draft, isn't it?" A smile spread over her face and she said with amusement, "No, Elling, it just seems longer!" She got to work on it again, and it was published in 1948. Brooks Atkinson of *The New York Times* wrote of it in

The American Scholar, "It has made the most profound impression on me . . . *Witness to the Truth* is the most illuminating book on Christ and Christianity that I have ever read."

Her life in Washington was very full. Edith made some lifelong friends as well as a vast number of acquaintances. We gave many parties—New Year's Eve parties, Election parties, and just parties. Edith was always the center.

Her breadth of interests was wide. She enjoyed talking with or listening to almost any intelligent person on practically any subject. But, if she got tired as the night went on she would do her "disappearing act." Her form of relaxation was not idle chitchat or sitting around; she much preferred a good detective story in a quiet room. She once said in astonishment to a highly intelligent young girl who never read detective stories, "You don't know *The Red Thumbmark* or *Whose Body?* Why, Dorna, you might just as well tell me you have never heard of *Hamlet!*" She thought the English stories superior to ours. She liked Austin Freeman and his detective, Dr. Thorndyke. She liked Agatha Christie, Patricia Wentworth, Ngaio Marsh, and Dorothy Sayers when she was still writing detective stories. She particularly liked Josephine Tey. She did not care at all for "rough stuff." She once said to a friend, "I like my murderers to be ladies and gentlemen!"

Many people of distinction would visit Washington and come to pay their respects to Edith. Isak Dinesen,

Arnold Toynbee, and Dr. Suzuki, the famous Zen Buddhist, often called on her. Robert Frost, Stephen Spender, and Robert Lowell occasionally came around. I remember when she was expecting Mr. Lowell she bought a book of his poems to bone up, as she was not familiar with his work. She told him, to his amusement, that there were some of his lines she could not understand and then said that the only line of modern poetry that stuck in her mind was: "We are the eyelids of defeated caves." "I know the man who wrote that," said Mr. Lowell. "Oh," exclaimed Edith, clapping her hands, "then you can tell me what it means." Mr. Lowell replied thoughtfully, "No, I can't. But when I see him I will ask him." Edith then enjoyed herself speculating on how it would be if one followed around the numerous modern poets to ask them what they were talking about.

Many people would drop in for tea or cocktails. In a letter to me a friend of Edith's wrote, "Do you remember, surely not so vividly as I do, the time Miss Hamilton's dog jumped on me as I was sitting in your living room drinking tea. I held on to my cup and saucer but the dog jostled me and I spilt some tea on my trouser leg. Instantly Miss Hamilton, then in her late eighties, leapt to her feet and moved like a sandpiper to the hall and down the steps to the basement floor. In no time she returned with a bowl of water and a rag and there and then knelt upon the floor in front of me and daubed away at my trouser leg where the tea had wet it. Quick, efficient strokes and without interrupting whatever we were talking about, no fuss about how awful of the dog, etc.

"Then she straightened up quick and sharp as a jack knife and returned to the basement with the bowl of water and cloth. When she came back it was as if nothing at all had happened. And nothing at all had except this demonstration of her kindliness, her simplicity and her athletic prowess."

John L. Lewis came often for dinner. When Edith was convalescing from her broken hip he would go up and sit beside her bed and every now and then say a sentence in Latin to his own amusement. We, in the drawing room, could hear bursts of laughter coming down the stairs from them both.

When Ezra Pound was in St. Elizabeth's Hospital, a friend of his took Edith out to see him. He said that he was lonely. For quite a while she called on him every week. He was then writing the China part of his *Cantos*, and he found in Edith an especially receptive listener, for she had a great interest in China. As time went on, Pound was visited by prominent writers from all over the world, including young aspiring poets who went to the hospital to sit at his feet and listen to him thunder. Edith would sometimes take a poet out in her car and bring him back. She once said to me, "I told the boy that I thought some of Mr. Pound's couplets were truly beautiful but a large part of his writing was incomprehensible. He looked at me pityingly!"

Edith was tremendously sympathetic with the effort

that was being made to set Pound free. She felt that to keep him in St. Elizabeth's was not only idiotic, it was unjust. But his way of writing was hardly up her alley.

The person who was nearest to Edith and who gave her the greatest intellectual stimulus was Huntington Cairns, the secretary-treasurer and general counsel of the National Gallery of Art. Shortly after we got to Washington he asked to come to see Edith as he was writing his book *The Limits of Art* and wanted to quote from something she had written. They made an instant close connection that lasted throughout Edith's life. In an interview with the *Washington Star* in 1965 Huntington said, "I saw Edith Hamilton nearly every Sunday night for twenty years." He frequently came with his wife, Florence, to whom Edith was also devoted.

By the time we left New York Edith's reputation as a classicist and author was already widely established. But the honorary degrees from various universities and colleges, the numerous awards, her election to the American Academy of Arts and Letters, having her books translated into various languages throughout the world, all came after we had moved to Washington.

When we left New York in 1943, Edith was seventy-six and by any normal standards she was old. But, as it turned out, she had twenty years ahead of her of writing and publishing. She was indeed "ageless." During this period she wrote three more books, *Witness to the Truth*, *Spokesmen for God*, and *The Echo of Greece*, and twenty-eight introductions to the Dialogues of

Plato. She gave a number of addresses and wrote essays and book reviews. She would never consent to review a book unless she was prepared really to study it. As has been said, she never "tossed off" anything.

In 1952 William Faulkner won the Nobel Prize. Edith had read a few of his books, thought little of them, and considered writing an article about him. She obtained and read everything he had had published and then settled down to write. The fact that Faulkner had become enormously popular and widely publicized affected Edith not at all. She wrote to a friend, "I have been writing an article on Faulkner. Why? It was a concern on my spirit, that is all I can say." Every subject she took up was essentially a "concern on her spirit."

The conclusion of her essay "Goethe and Faust" is, in another way, revealing of Edith. She describes the last scene of the first part of *Faust* and the, to her, astonishing beginning and substance of the second part. Gretchen has dropped out of sight. Edith writes, "What is the explanation of this strange refusal on the part of one of the world's greatest writers to complete what he began with such power of truth and beauty? No character in literature surpasses Gretchen in point of pathos. But Goethe turned away from her so decisively that he did not allow one thought of her ever again to enter Faust's mind. Apparently it never occurred to him that Faust might thereby forfeit the reader's sympathy. The play says beyond the possiblity of doubt that Goethe thought leaving Gretchen to die and forgetting her was entirely comprehensible. . . . The only way to love without danger, Spinoza declared, was to love with never a pang to trouble the spirit, was 'to give love to that which is eternal and infinite, to that which alone causes joy untainted by any sorrow.' That was the way Goethe could love, secure in the infinite and eternal against which is the lot of those who love through sickness and through sin, through danger and through death, individual people in this finite and temporal world."

Edith then quotes what Schiller wrote of Goethe, "He binds men to him by small as well as by great attentions, but he always knows how to hold himself free." Edith concludes her essay, "He never gave himself. He never really suffered. . . . There will always be men to commend this remarkable achievement, hardly to be paralleled in human annals, the result of an unwavering resolution to avoid pain and complete clarity of mind to perceive the one sure way. . . . But there will always be others to maintain that this surpassing genius, power of intellect and power of poetry combined as in hardly another, refused 'the great initiation.' That refusal made *Faust* what it is. Goethe turned away from the tragic heights Faust might have trod, and he never saw to what low levels he made him sink."

In Edith's chapter on St. Paul in *Witness to the Truth* she quotes his beautiful statements about the love of God and then writes, "But greater still than these great expressions of divine love is what he wrote of love here on earth. . . . What he wrote is brief, only thir-

1892: Edith at Bryn Mawr College

1916: Edith at the
Bryn Mawr School

*1922: Winter at Sea Wall in front of our house —
Edith with Dorian and our pets*

1929: Sharing a picnic lunch at Sunion

*1929: Edith with me in front of the Erectheum
and, at right, Edith on the steps of the Parthenon*

1936: While living at Gramercy Park

Edith receives the scroll from the Mayor of Athens making her an honorary citizen

Addressing the audience —

*"I am a citizen of Athens . . .
this is the proudest
moment of my life."*

Receiving sprays of laurel from two Greek girls in costume

With Edith, the Mayor of Athens, U.S. Ambassador Allen, and Mr. Achilles Yerocostopoulos, the Greek Minister of Education

1962: Our home at Sea Wall

Across the bluebells to the mountains

Setting the stage *The show begins*

1958 — EDITH CONFRONTS TELEVISION

Conversation piece with Huntington Cairns

Back on the porch — conversation continued

1958: Edith with Mary's children

Isaak Dinesen in our Washington home

1961: On the porch at Sea Wall in her favorite chair

1962: In Washington — Doris Fielding Reid, the author

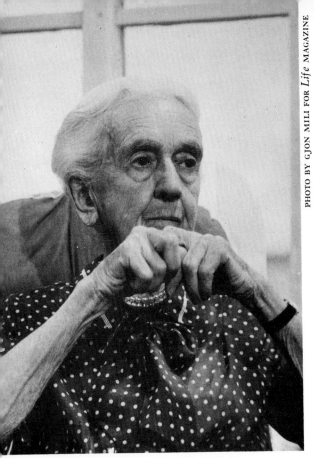

1961: Two studies of Edith, taken at Sea Wall

"*All my vague miseries I feel will be dispersed by the sea winds.*"

teen short verses, hardly a quarter of a page, and yet all
of human love is there, its pre-eminence and the pain it is
bound up with. Apart from it nothing men do is worth
anything: 'The tongues of men and of angels' are 'as
sounding brass or a tinkling cymbal.' The mind, reason,
knowledge, are profitless. 'Though I understand all mys-
teries, and all knowledge, and have not love I am nothing.' 'Whether there be prophecies they shall fail.
Whether there be tongues they shall cease, whether
there be knowledge it shall vanish away,' but love will
endure. Without it faith, the very cornerstone of the
church, is of no account: 'Though I have all faith so that
I could remove mountains and have not love, I am nothing.' So too the very utmost of self-sacrifice: 'Though I
bestow all my goods to feed the poor, and though I give
my body to be burned, and have not love, it profiteth me
nothing.' 'Love suffereth long and is kind; Love thinketh
no evil; seeketh not her own; beareth all things, believeth
all things, hopeth all things, endureth all things. Love
never faileth. And now abideth faith, hope, love, these
three; but the greatest of these is love.' "

Edith often spoke of the fact that the word "love"
was sometimes translated by "charity." She said that the
Greek word could be translated either way. She felt,
however, that the use of the word charity in the thir-
teenth chapter of the First Corinthians would obviously
destroy the meaning of one of the most inspired passages
in the Bible.

These two quotations throw a light on Edith herself.

They explain, at least in part, the devotion she gave and inspired. She did not "refuse the great initiation." To her, St. Paul was clearly writing about "love on earth."

In the spring of 1954 after a very short illness my mother died. She was ninety-two years old but her mind and her sense of fun were as keen as they had always been. She had lived with us in Washington for ten years and her death changed our household drastically. As Christmas approached Edith said over and over, "It seems so pointless without your mother." My mother's chauffeur-houseman had always brought us a tree and many branches of holly from his farm in Virginia. He had the unfortunate desire to trim the tree and decorate the house himself, and my mother found much amusement in watching our rather futile efforts to circumvent him. For years Elling Aannestad came down from New York every Christmas, spent two nights with us, and was part of the "opening of presents" festivity which took place after breakfast; later we had our midday Christmas dinner.

Our first Christmas alone was hard to take. Although we were devoted to him, we had let the chauffeur go. Elling was in Europe, and with my mother gone neither Edith nor I seemed to care enough to do anything about the day. A perceptive friend invited us over for Christmas dinner, and when I asked Edith if she wanted to go she said, "Oh, yes. I don't want to face this empty house on Christmas." Edith had grown to love Washington and the friends she had made there, and after my mother's death she often spoke, with deep gratitude, of the "warmth of feeling" that surrounded us. "They are real *friends*," she would say, "and you know I don't use that word lightly."

In 1956 I had been at Loomis, Sayles for twenty-seven years and I decided I would ask for seven weeks' vacation, which was ungrudgingly granted. Neither Edith nor I had been out of the country since our trip to Greece in 1929 and we decided to go abroad. Edith said she had never seen Etna and had always longed to. We planned to go by boat to Sicily; motor from Palermo to Taormina, where Edith could feast her eyes on Etna; fly to Rome for a few days; and end up in Madrid—Edith had never been to Spain. I think that many of us, particularly as we grow older, like best to revisit the places where we have been in the past. Edith did not. She wanted to go where she had never been before.

We were very excited about our plan. Edith said, "Doris, do you *realize* how long it has been since I have taken a trip? The last time was with Dorian when he was eleven years old. Now he is thirty-eight." Senator and Mrs. Ralph Flanders, of whom Edith was very fond, brought us information about Taormina, where they had often been, and told us to stay at the Timeo Hotel, which was high up by the Greek theater and had an unobstructed view of Etna. "Oh, *what* fun this is going to be!" Edith said, clapping her hands.

We set sail from New York in February and gave a cocktail party on the ship for the many friends who had come to see us off. While they were drinking a toast, a friend whispered to me, "Isn't it impossible to believe that Edith is eighty-nine years old?" It was indeed.

The ocean voyage was delightful. The H. V. Kaltenborns were on the ship and added greatly to our enjoyment. Sicily came up to, in fact exceeded, our expectations. The surprising beauty of the drive from Palermo to Taormina was marred by the possibility, indeed probability, that we would be killed at any moment! Our Sicilian driver sped like mad up and down the narrow mountain passes and whirled with equal speed around hairpin turns. Edith maintained that he put his hand on his horn as we left the hotel and kept it there until we reached Taormina eight hours later.

Edith often sat by her bedroom window contemplating Etna, or walking around the Greek theater, from which there was also a superb view of the mountain. Once when we were sitting in the lounge someone shouted, "Etna is erupting." We looked up and saw sheets of fire and smoke pouring out of the top of that incredible volcano. It was a dramatic and awesome sight. The newspapers reported that it was the first time Etna had erupted in fifty years.

I had assumed that Edith would want to go to Syracuse, where the Greek soldiers had died in the quarries, but she had no desire to do so. She said, "It won't have any resemblance to what it looked like hundreds and hundreds of years ago. And you know I have never had any interest in historic spots. I mean the place where, say, some famous character was assassinated or where a vital treaty was signed. The truth is, I expect I have no historical imagination and the few places of this kind that I have seen had no intrinsic beauty."

When we reached Rome, Francesca Palmer joined us. She had been staying in Paris and the main topic of conversation was the weather. The early part of 1956 was noteworthy for the unprecedented cold throughout Europe. Sicily had been exceedingly cold. Francesca told us stories about the mess Paris was in, with the lack of heat and broken, frozen water pipes. One morning Edith read to us out of a newspaper, "Madrid is colder than it has been for a hundred years." Edith said she did not want to be colder than she had been for a hundred years. So we decided to change our plans, skip Spain, spend further time in Italy, fly to Portugal, and go home from there.

To Edith the trip was a joy from start to finish. The fact that we always had to be bundled up in heavy winter coats did not detract from her delight in Orvieto, Assisi, Perugia, Florence, Pisa, and so on. She added greatly to Francesca's and my enjoyment by telling us vivid stories about St. Francis of Assisi and others. I remember once going into a chapel and Edith started talking in Latin to a young priest, to his great surprise and enjoyment. He could not speak a word of English.

While we were over there Edith had a letter from her sister Alice urging her to stay abroad longer than we had planned. Alice wrote, "After all you won't be going

abroad again." Edith read this aloud to me in bewilder-
ment. "Can you imagine why Alice thinks I won't be
taking another trip?" she exclaimed. I answered, "I expect she is considering that you will be ninety in a little
over a year." "Oh," was the extent of Edith's reply. As
it turned out, this was the first of four trips to Europe
we took in the next years.

"A Citizen of Athens"

⁊ THE YEAR 1957 was one of major events. It started off when Edith went out shopping in the pouring rain, attempted to jump over a gutter flooded with water, fell, and broke her pelvis. She was in traction for six weeks and when she first got up out of bed she was very weak indeed. She said her legs seemed to be made of spaghetti. It was clear that it would take her some time to regain her strength and get her feet back under her. The monotony was broken by the publication of her seventh book, *The Echo of Greece*, and reading reviews that kept coming in from all over the world.

Then John Latimer, president of the Classical Association of the Atlantic States, told her that the Association was celebrating its fiftieth anniversary in New York in the spring, and asked if she would go up and make an address for the occasion. The idea seemed impossible. Edith then could not take one step without considerable assistance. When her doctor called, Edith told him of the project and asked him if he thought it reasonable to assume that she would be fit by spring. The doctor sat looking at the floor for a minute, then he turned to me and said, "Well, seeing it's Miss Edith, very likely she will be." She was. She went to New York in April and made her speech. The next day Brendan Gill came to interview her and wrote a delightful piece for *The New Yorker* which he entitled "Nineteen and A Half Minutes." Edith had said, in answer to one of his questions, that she thought long speeches on such occasions were so tiresome and that she had determined to talk no longer than twenty minutes. Actually, she said, it came out at nineteen and a half minutes. Of *The Echo of Greece* Mr. Gill wrote that it had "received universally favorable reviews ('masterly,' 'edifying' and 'beguiling' were among the adjectives most commonly applied to it), and its sales are maintaining a lively pace. So, for that matter, is its author, who came to town the other day to deliver a speech before the Classical Association. . . . Miss Hamilton happens to be eighty-nine and is therefore one of the most venerable of current writers and speech-makers, but while we were in her presence it never occurred to us to reflect on the fact that she was born just after the Civil War. Miss Hamilton is as beautiful and wise a person as we have ever met, and we feel sure that her beauty and intelligence have been heightened rather than diminished by the years."

Early in May Storer Lunt, her old friend who, following Warder Norton's death, became president of W. W. Norton & Company, called me up to say there was a project on to give a performance that summer in Athens of her translation of the *Prometheus Bound*. The Greek government wanted to know if Edith could come to Athens and attend as their guest of honor. Mr. Lunt, who knew that she had had a rugged winter and also that she would be ninety years old that summer, asked me if I thought she was up to making the trip. I said, "Sure she is," or something to that effect. He asked me to say nothing about this to Edith until all the arrangements had been definitely completed. I then watched Edith, as was her usual custom, make out extensive grocery and supply lists for Sea Wall, engage a cook for the summer and invite friends to come for visits. I finally received the go-ahead sign from Storer and when I got back from the office that afternoon and we were having tea, I started by saying that her translation of the *Prometheus* was going to be given in Athens. Edith said, "Oh, I got a letter some months ago from a Mr. James Elliott saying he would like to produce my translation of the *Prometheus* in Athens. But I did not suppose he would be able to and I forgot all about it. Well, that is very nice, isn't it?" She then put on her glasses and picked up the evening paper. I said, "Edith Hamilton, will you please put that paper down and *listen* to me." I then told her that Greece was inviting her to come to Athens as the guest of the Greek government. They would bring her over on the Greek liner S.S. *Queen Frederika* sailing on July 11. During her stay in Athens she would be the guest of the government. Edith looked really startled. "Go to Athens!" she exclaimed. "It seems mad." "Be that as it may," I replied, "here is the invitation. Do you want to go?" She turned and looked out of the window for a few moments. A smile spread over her face, then she laughed and said, "Of course I'll go."

Shortly thereafter the following press release was sent to the newspapers from the United States Delphic Festival Committee:

"PROMETHEUS BOUND" FOR GREECE

Robert W. Dowling, Chairman of the Board of ANTA, announces that the President's Special International Program for cultural presentations (administered by ANTA as the professional agency of the State Department), in cooperation with the Greek Ministry for Education, will sponsor James S. Elliott's production of Aeschylus' *Prometheus Bound* in Athens. The event will take place in the ancient theatre of Herodes Atticus, situated at the foot of the Acropolis, during the last week of July.

Edith Hamilton's translation will be used and the Greek government will take this opportunity to pay tribute to the celebrated American and Philhellene, for her contributions toward fostering Greek culture. Miss Hamilton, now nearing 90 years of age, had her recent book, *The Echo of Greece*, published in January. She will sail for Athens with the American actors aboard the S.S. *Queen Frederika* on July 11th.

Honorary Chairman

Edith Hamilton

Honorary Committee

Judith Anderson	Maxwell Anderson	Clarence Derwent
Paul Muni	George Melas	Elsa Maxwell
Helen Hayes	Fredric March	Tennessee Williams
Christian Palamas		Spyros Skouras

Immediately afterward, the newspapers began telephoning to ask Edith for interviews. Practically every-

where she went her picture was snapped and published
in some paper. Newspapers throughout the country
wrote columns concerning the project. Mr. Elliott came
to call, bringing Mr. Bourlos, a distinguished Greek
actor, to discuss the coming performance. "This is all too
ridiculous," Edith said to me. "After all, *Aeschylus*
wrote the *Prometheus.*"

The *Queen Frederika* was to sail at midnight and her
publishers gave an enormous party in honor of Edith on
board the ship before it sailed. More champagne was
consumed than I had thought possible. This time Edith
did not do her "disappearing act."

We had a delightful voyage over. Several of our intimate friends decided that they were not going to miss
this unique event and came over on the boat with us.
Edith had never before been in such luxurious quarters
on an ocean liner. They gave her the Delphi Suite,
which consisted of a double bedroom and bath that led
into a charming sitting room.

With the exception of Mr. Bourlos, Edith had not
met any members of the cast. Shortly after we sailed, the
actress Blanche Yurka called to see her. It transpired that
the cast thought that the *Prometheus* should be somewhat cut, and they feared that Edith, like most authors,
would refuse to have her translation abbreviated. Miss
Yurka had been chosen to broach this ticklish subject.
When she finally posed her question, Edith exclaimed,
"Cut! of course it should be cut. All the geography can
be left out." Then she picked up her copy of the play,

pointed to a paragraph here and a page or so there and said, "All this should be omitted." Miss Yurka interrupted, "Miss Hamilton, if you go on there won't be any play left." They both laughed and then Edith started to talk. She said that, as Miss Yurka knew, the *Prometheus* was not really a play as there was no action. It was essentially a recitation; it contained some of the most magnificent poetry ever written, and its theme was one of universal and timeless significance. She went on to say that there were parts that were undoubtedly of local interest and meaning to people living twenty-five hundred years ago, but to us today they were meaningless and boring. "*Of course*," she said, "your cast wants to cut the play. It must be cut."

Edith and Miss Yurka struck up a lasting connection. Miss Yurka, who was playing the part of Io, told her many stories which amused Edith greatly. I remember she once said that in the course of her acting career she had been offered a few poor roles, but this was the first time she had been asked to play the part of a cow.

Edith had been informed that Nicolo Tucci was going over on our boat, as *The New Yorker* had asked him to write her profile. Edith saw a lot of Mr. Tucci. He told her of the various interesting and distinguished figures he had known, and gave her a most vivid account of Toscanini's last days. He told her of his own childhood and early youth and read her parts of the autobiography he was writing. Edith enjoyed him very much, but to her great amusement, he never seemed to get around to the profile of her that he was supposed to be writing. A year or so later he called on Edith in New York, bringing his wife. He started in his usual animated fashion describing some incident in his life, when Edith said, "You know, Mrs. Tucci, I think I will write a profile of your husband." Mr. Tucci burst into a roar of laughter. "It's all your fault, Miss Hamilton," he said, "you are such an inspired listener." Edith replied, "Not at all. What you said to me was far more interesting than anything I could have said to you." It was a gay afternoon.

Edith got to know the whole cast, who were exceedingly friendly. Mr. Elliott joined our boat at Crete and he was Jimmy by the time we reached the Piraeus.

We were told that the ship would dock at 8:00 P.M. and everyone packed up ready to disembark. Actually, we did not reach the harbor until about 1:30 A.M. For some reason there was a furor about getting our luggage off the boat and we did not reach our hotel, the Grande Bretagne, until after three o'clock that morning. Elling Aannestad and Francesca Palmer had flown over to join us in Athens and they stayed up half the night to greet us when we finally arrived at the hotel. Edith seemed as fresh and cheerful as if it were five o'clock in the afternoon. "What is Edith *made* of?" said Francesca.

That afternoon there was a plan for us all to go up on the Acropolis at sunset. It was a divine day, but I suggested to Edith that she put off taking the climb as she must be tired—I certainly was. But Edith said no, that this was an afternoon in a hundred and we might not have another. She was so right. Although we went up on the Acropolis a number of times while we were in Athens, that windless evening, with the astonishing beauty of the sunset, was not to be duplicated. Many members of the cast and several distinguished individuals made this special trip up to the Acropolis with us. Elling was walking with Edith when she suddenly grabbed his arm and said, "Don't leave me. Stay and talk to that literary gentleman I see approaching. He is going to expect me to say something profound."

The date for the performance of the *Prometheus* had been changed from the end of July to August 8, and Edith and I and several of our friends decided to take a motor trip. We went to Delphi, Olympia, Epidaurus, and Corinth. It was the same trip that Edith, Dorian, and I had taken in 1929 and Edith said, "This is Greece revisited, but I had not quite remembered the surpassing beauty."

When we got back to Athens the festivities began. There were cocktail parties, luncheon parties and receptions given in Edith's honor; the red carpet was out. Storer Lunt had flown over from America to join us and he also squired Edith around. George Allen, then our ambassador to Greece, took me aside and told me that King Paul was going to bestow upon her the Gold Cross of the Legion of Benefaction, and just before the *Prometheus* opened the Mayor would take Edith onto the stage and pronounce her a citizen of Athens. I was not to tell Edith about this, as it was to be a surprise. I told Mr. Allen that that would never do. Edith would not hear just what was being said and would not know who was presenting her with what. Mr. Allen reluctantly agreed.

That evening when I told Edith of the honors she was about to receive, she grew very serious and said, "You know, Doris, this is all wrong. These awards should be given to Gilbert Murray. The only reason why I am getting them, and the explanation for all this newspaper publicity, is because I am ninety years old. That makes a good story." "Well," I said, "Gilbert Murray will be ninety years old this summer. You will have to think up something else." As my remarks were unanswerable she just said to me, "You are a goose," and that ended that conversation!

Edith received the following invitation:

THE MINISTER OF NATIONAL EDUCATION
MR. ACHILLES YEROCOSTOPOULOS
REQUESTS THE PLEASURE OF YOUR COMPANY
AT A LUNCHEON IN HONOR OF
THE DISTINGUISHED SCHOLAR AND AUTHOR
MISS EDITH HAMILTON
PRESIDENT OF THE UNITED STATES DELPHIC FESTIVAL
COMMEMORATION COMMITTEE

When she read it, she said that this was the first she had heard of her being president of the U.S.D.F.C.C. and asked if I had been told of it. I answered that I had not, and it rather looked as though she were being ignored! At the close of this luncheon she was presented with the Gold Cross of the Legion of Benefaction, which Mr. Yerocostopoulos pinned upon her.

The Mayor of Athens gave her a delightful reception. She met Madame Tsaldaris, who was the only woman ever to be a member of the Greek Cabinet. Madame Tsaldaris talked in modern Greek, Edith talked in English, and they both talked at the same time. It was a very spirited occasion.

Edith knew that when she received the scroll making her a Citizen of Athens she would have to say something in acknowledgment. She had never been in the theater of Herodes Atticus and she wanted to take a look at it and see where she would be standing. That huge open-air amphitheater beneath the Acropolis was empty when we went in and as she stood looking up at those tiers and tiers of stone benches which seated over four thousand and which seemed to extend right up into the sky, it was somehow overwhelming. "I don't think I can speak here. Do you?" she said to me. "Frankly, no," I answered helpfully. Then I climbed up to the very top seats, having told her that when I waved she should start talking. I waved. She talked, and I could hear her clearly and easily. On the way home I remarked that those old Greeks certainly understood the problems of acoustics better than we did. She laughed and said, "Well, an ancient Greek said that the earth moved around the sun sixteen hundred years before Copernicus thought of it."

Over the years Edith received many honorary degrees and awards, but the honor she most deeply cared about was when she was made a Citizen of Athens.

On our arrival at the theater on the night of the performance of the *Prometheus*, Edith was escorted by the Mayor of Athens, Ambassador Allen, Duncan Emerick, our Cultural Attaché, and an exceedingly handsome Greek dignitary whose name I do not remember. I was instructed to go straight into the theater and sit in the front row. It was a clear, starlit night and the Herodes Atticus was full to overflowing. The audience in the top rows looked as though they were sitting in the middle of the Milky Way.

When Edith came on, there was a thunder of applause. With an amused and interested smile she was looking around to see for whom they were clapping when the ambassador, who was escorting her, leaned down and said, "Bow, Miss Hamilton, *bow*. The applause is for you." The Mayor then led her onto the stage and, after a citation, presented her with a scroll which made her a Citizen of Athens. She stepped briskly to a microphone which had been installed and made the following brief speech with, as usual, no notes.

"It is impossible for me to express my gratitude for the honors shown me. I am a Citizen of Athens, of the city I have for so long loved as much as I love my own country. This is the proudest moment of my life. And yet as I stand here speaking to you under the very shadow of the Acropolis a deeper feeling rises. I see Athens, the home of beauty and of thought. Even today among buildings, the Parthenon is supreme, Plato's thought has never been transcended; of the four great tragedians, three are Greek. We are here to see a performance of the *Prometheus*. In all literature, Prometheus is the great rebel against tyranny. It is most fitting that he should be presented to the world now, in this period of the world's history, and here, in the city of Athens. For Athens, truly the mother of beauty and of thought, is also the mother of freedom. Freedom was a Greek discovery. The Greeks were the first free nation in the world. In the *Prometheus* they have sent a ringing call down through the centuries to all who would be free. Prometheus, confronted with the utmost tyranny, will not submit. He tells the tyrant's messenger, who urges him to yield, 'Go and persuade the sea-wave not to break. You will persuade me no more easily.' That is the spirit Greece gave to the world. It challenges us and we need the challenge. Greece rose to the very height not because she was big, she was very small; not because she was rich, she was very poor; not even because she was wonderfully gifted. She rose because there was in the Greeks the greatest spirit that moves in humanity, the spirit that makes men free. It is impossible for us to believe that, of all the nations of the world, Greece was the only one that had the vision of what St. John in the Gospels calls 'the true light' which, he adds, 'lightest every man who cometh into the world'; but we know that she was the only one who followed it. She kept on—on what one of her poets calls 'the long and rough and steep road.' Therefore her light was never extinguished.

Therefore we are met tonight to see a play which has lived for twenty-five hundred years. In those years the Greeks have been outstripped by science and technology, but never in the love of the truth, never in the creation of beauty and of freedom."

These words were extraordinarily moving. The depth of Edith's feeling and conviction came through. *The New York Times,* describing the event, wrote, "The crowd showed itself to be moved by Miss Hamilton's appearance. In a brief speech she referred to freedom as a Greek discovery . . . . The ninety-year-old white-haired author was the evening's leading attraction and what followed her appearance on the stage seemed anticlimactic."

Later, when Storer Lunt was telling her how magnificent she had been, she laughingly said, "Well, did you hear my knees banging together when I began to talk?"

Of this event *Publishers' Weekly* wrote, "While Edith Hamilton addressed this crowded amphitheatre of Herodes Atticus, floodlights in her honor were thrown on the Parthenon, the Temple of Zeus and, for the first time in history, the Stoa. . . . We can think of no other of the year's literary events that could be more moving and dramatic than this."

The performance of the *Prometheus* was disappointing. Mr. Bourlos, who took the part of Prometheus, spoke in modern Greek. The rest of the cast, all Americans, did their parts in English. *Time* magazine wrote, "Though the performance was a bit too complicated to arouse noisy enthusiasm Miss Hamilton's appearance more than made the evening."

After the show was over the actors and Edith were surrounded by many people offering congratulations. A succession of photographers from magazines and newspapers took pictures from every conceivable angle. When we left the theater many of our friends came back with us to the Grande Bretagne, where we had nightcaps, toasted Edith, and discussed the performance. Everyone wanted to know what Edith thought of it. She seemed to be dodging the subject and then she suddenly said, "You know, dear people, a deaf person has to make an effort to hear in the theater. I know the *Prometheus* practically by heart and, to be perfectly frank, I did not try to hear them recite it. You say that Mr. Bourlos talked in Greek and the rest of the cast answered him in English. That strikes me as a poor idea." She stopped, laughed, and said, "Now you see, being hard of hearing has its advantages."

We had decided to fly home. There were then no Greek transatlantic airlines and apparently, although the Greek government felt responsible for Edith's safety bringing her over, she could kill herself on the way back if she felt like it. In those prejet days the trip took twenty-three hours and we boarded a Pan American plane with Storer Lunt, who accompanied us. We landed at Idlewild early on the morning of August 12, Edith's ninetieth birthday. "Let's fly straight to Sea Wall," Edith said. So we took a taxi over to La Guardia;

there a *New York Herald Tribune* reporter lay in wait and asked for an interview.

He wrote in his column, which appeared the next morning, that Edith was "of lively wit," that she commented on the gallantry of European men and, looking amusedly at a photographer during the interview, said, "I am so puffed up with attention. I am surprised that you gentlemen didn't kiss my hand."

The *Washington Post* wrote in an editorial about her: "Yesterday one of our most distinguished townswomen celebrated her 90th birthday anniversary. Miss Edith Hamilton is beyond much doubt the most remarkable American lady of letters; and not the least remarkable of her qualities is that her intellectual powers seem to have increased rather than diminished with the years. Her most recent book, *The Echo of Greece*, shows her to be still the mistress of an English prose style virtually without contemporary counterpart in its simplicity, clarity and beauty. Her physical vigor is scarcely less astonishing, and was shown in her recent journey to her beloved Athens where she was the figure of honor at a performance of the *Prometheus Bound* of Aeschylus in her own English version in the ancient amphitheatre beneath the Acropolis."

The Sunday *Chicago Tribune* devoted its column "The Literary Spotlight" to her. "Tomorrow will be the 90th birthday of Miss Edith Hamilton, who has more than once been described as the wisest of womankind." It spoke of the fact that *The Echo of Greece* together with *The Greek Way* were the dual choice of the judges of the Book-of-the-Month Club for their summer Book Dividend. "So, Edith Hamilton, after watching the presentation of her translation of Aeschylus in the ancient theatre of Herodes Attitcus, after being feted and honored as the guest of the Greek government, will return to find herself, on her 90th birthday, the author of best sellers. . . . Many more happy birthdays, Edith Hamilton!"

In her interview at La Guardia, she spoke of some writing she had in mind, and then she added, "But I am not going to do it now. I am going up to my summer home on Mt. Desert and lie on the rocks and watch the tide." We caught the next plane to Maine and reached Sea Wall that afternoon.

Speaking, Traveling, Writing

ON OUR arrival in Sea Wall, my niece, Mary, greeted Edith with a ninetieth-birthday present: two tiny and particularly sprightly kittens. Edith named them Nip and Tuck, and, of course, adored them.

By then there were only a few weeks left of the summer and Edith announced that she was going to do nothing at all except sit on the rocks and watch the ocean, take walks with her dog, and play with the kittens. "As for writing," she said, "I am never going to write another line." One of us reminded her that that was exactly what she had said when she finished *The Greek Way* some thirty years ago. Another remarked that whenever Edith finished *any* piece of writing she always said that she would never write again. Edith interrupted, smiling, "Well, now, let's talk about something interesting. Do look at the bluebells."

Edith had a great love of flowers but, with the exception of wild flowers, which particularly appealed to her, she wanted them in the house. She had no interest in gardening of any kind. Once, when a caller at Sea Wall was telling her about his flower beds and small vegetable garden, he asked her why she had put her house on that very rocky point. "Because," she replied, laughing, "nothing will grow here." One summer, however, she planted a few bluebells in the patches of earth between the rocks. None came up the next season and she assumed that they had died. The following summer, several blossoms appeared and she led the children up to them saying that on no account must they be picked as they might spread. As the years went by they sprang up in an astonishingly wide radius and finally the month of August was a joy with what Edith called "that rapturous blue." Few people talked of Sea Wall without speaking of "Edith's bluebells."

Shortly after we returned to Washington Edith received a letter from the National Broadcasting Company asking her if she would give a talk on "our joint Center for Educational Television program to be given at the Metropolitan Museum in New York, on October 30th." Edith said that would give her very little time to prepare her talk, but she accepted.

The show was to be staged in the basement of the museum and a rehearsal was scheduled for a day or so in advance. After arriving at the Metropolitan, Edith walked for what seemed to be blocks before she reached the steep, narrow stairs which led down to the designated place of action. She was put on a little wooden chair and there she sat while the elaborate scenery was put in place and while they discussed who was to say what and when. She made her talk and then a few men did a dance entitled "Chaos." While these poor fellows were rehearsing their performance, Greek statues were brought in upside down, on rollers. If the idea was to portray "chaos" they could not have done a better job.

A room was set aside upstairs for Edith's friends and anybody else who was interested, where there was a television screen on which bits of the rehearsal were shown. Apparently many people were interested because the room was packed and cocktails were served. I suddenly thought that the least I could do would be to take a cocktail down to Edith. I was stopped in the middle of those dreadful little stairs and told that no liquor could be served in the basement. I asked if I might bring her a glass of sherry. The answer was no.

Be all that as it may, the program was a real success. No effort was spared in arranging the setting. Those superb Greek statues were carefully placed and were most effective. A gentleman said to me, "Miss Hamilton looked so handsome." When I repeated this remark to Edith she said, "Well, I certainly had a lot of competition, standing by the statue of the Apollo Belvedere."

Edith had a letter from the producer saying, "You were positively superb yesterday. . . . National Broadcasting Company's manager of public service programs telephoned from St. Louis to say how wonderful your comments were. You were magnificent." Then the producer added, "You were also a real trouper in meeting the exigencies of live television." She certainly was that!

When we returned to Washington, Robert Richman, president of the Institute of Contemporary Arts, asked

Edith if she would deliver one of the lectures in the Institute's distinguished series. While she was considering the proposition I was looking over their annual statement of speakers. "There is quite an assembly here from all over the world," I said. "Here are Julian and Aldous Huxley, Jacques Maritain, Salvador Madariaga, Paul Tillich, T. S. Eliot, Frank Lloyd Wright." "Oh, Doris," Edith interrupted, "I am not interested in all those names. I am just considering whether I have anything I want to say that is worth saying."

She accepted the invitation and the lecture was scheduled for January, 1958. It was to begin at 8:30 and a group of her friends who went with us suggested that we get there early, the idea being that we would thereby procure for ourselves choice seats. When we arrived a little after eight, the hall, which seated about nine hundred, was packed. There was not a seat left and there were already a few standees about. Edith had been met on arrival and whisked off somewhere and one of our enterprising friends who had come down from New York for the occasion got a table out of the foyer, put it in the back of the hall against the wall, and on this we sat throughout the lecture. I was told afterward that they let in a hundred standees and then closed the doors.

It was an unusually keen and responsive audience, and Edith was in top form. After Mr. Richman had introduced her, she stepped to the lecture desk and said, "I know Mr. Richman has been saying nice things about me but I am so hard of hearing that I don't know what they were. But I want to thank him for them and say how honored I feel that I, a woman of ninety, should be asked to speak before the Institute of *Contemporary* Arts." There was much laughter and applause and then Edith got down to her subject, which was focused essentially on education. None of what she said, either witty or serious, escaped the audience, and Mr. Richman had had the perspicacity to make a tape recording of it, which I did not know of until after Edith's death. And now, eight years after the lecture was given, a commercial record of it has been made.

When the lecture was over, many friends came back to our house and compliments were being showered on Edith when Mr. Richman said, "I have a complaint to make. I asked you to talk for about an hour and you finished up in slightly under forty-five minutes." "Now, Robert," Edith replied, "admit, *admit* that my talk was long enough."

After our guests had left, Edith said to me, "Doris, will you tell me honestly, truthfully, was my lecture any good?" "How idiotic can you get?" I replied. "You must know damned well—" Edith arose saying, "Don't start swearing. Now I am going to bed and try to get some sleep. There is no truth in you," she said, over her shoulder, smiling as she left the room.

In March, Edith was visiting in New York and was the speaker on a Martha Deane radio program. When she returned to Washington she said, "I will be ninety-one years old this summer and I have done all the work I am ever going to do. From now on I mean to enjoy my-self. Nothing more." Shortly thereafter the *Saturday Evening Post* wrote her that they were publishing a few essays, called *Adventures of the Mind*, by outstanding individuals in different fields and would she write one for this series. She said she would.

Remembering the remark she had made only a week or so previously, she felt some explanation was in order and she said that it would interest her to develop a theme that she had "dragged into" her talk at the Institute for Contemporary Arts. She reminded me of how important she had always felt was a study of the past. In one of her books she had written, "History repeats itself. The say-ing has become a truism; nevertheless, the study of the past is relegated to the scholar and the school-boy. And yet it is really a chart for our guidance—no less than that."

She entitled her essay "The Ever Present Past" and her first sentence read, "Is there an ever present past?" Two weeks before the essay appeared she had a brief note from the *Saturday Evening Post* saying, "We have changed your title to 'Lessons of the Past.'" This en-raged Edith and she immediately sent them a telegram. "I do not want my title changed. 'Lessons of the Past' sounds deadly tiresome and like a school book. It will put people off. Don't change my title." She never got an answer to this. The article appeared called "Lessons of the Past." When Edith got her copy of the magazine she just said characteristically, "Oh well," and turned her attention to something else. And she had something else to turn her attention to.

Huntington Cairns, who was on the board of the Bollingen Foundation told her that Bollingen wanted to get out the complete works of Plato in one volume. There was no complete one-volume Plato available in English. The idea was to choose the best British and the best American translations of the last century, from Jowett, the first edition of whose complete Plato came out in 1871, up to scholars of the present day.

The Bollingen Foundation wanted Edith to pick out the various translations and write an introduction to the book. Huntington and Edith talked at length about this project. Jowett was the only person who had translated all of Plato but they wanted to use as little as possible of this very familiar work. Huntington told Edith that she would not have to run around hunting for the various other translations, that he would procure them for her —a very handsome offer! I think that Bollingen and even Huntington assumed that Edith was familiar with all the translations, which she was not. It is hardly necessary to say that her absorption had always been with the original text. However, she said yes to the plan and went to work. A few weeks later when Huntington came over for the evening, Edith told him that she thought that the Dialogues should each have a brief introduction—not more than a page. Huntington said, "Splendid idea. You write them."

Edith agreed and afterward told me that when she

made this suggestion she had forgotten that Plato had written twenty-eight Dialogues. Later on she said that the longer she worked on this book the more she thought that a brief volume on Plato should be published at the same time that the collected works came out. She talked this over with Huntington, who was enthusiastic over the idea and said that of course she would write it as, in his opinion, no one else could. She and Huntington then agreed that if she would write the book on Plato, he would write the introduction to the Bollingen collection.

Edith worked for some three years on the Bollingen project. She read and studied innumerable translations of the Dialogues. She concluded that in many cases some were better than Jowett. She believed that Jowett's language was often stilted, whereas Socrates, she wrote, "had a great distaste for high-sounding talk." However, she often said that in the "purple passages" Jowett was the best. While she was working on the translations and writing her introductions to the Dialogues she was planning and making notes for her book on Plato.

During this period, her life went on as it always had. She saw many people. It was rare indeed that we sat down to tea or cocktails alone. Of course she did all the housekeeping. How she was ever able to do the writing she did remains a mystery to me.

In the spring of 1958 a big dinner was given in New York to present her with the Constance Lindsay Skinner Award. She gave a talk in acknowledgment and brief speeches were made about her by the United States Ambassador from Greece, George Melas; George Allen, then Director of the U.S.I.A.; and John Mason Brown, who began by saying that he had heard considerable criticism of Edith Hamilton because she had written a book on Greece when she had never been there. He continued, "After all, Dante wrote a highly thought of poem about the Inferno, where he certainly had never been." It was an unusually gay and delightful evening.

By this time I had retired from business and we decided to take a trip abroad and go to Spain. We wanted to get there well before the tourist season began and also before the hot weather descended. So on April 27 we took a night plane to Madrid where Rosamond Gilder and Francesca Palmer joined us, and our trip was a delight from start to finish.

Edith sent picture postcards almost daily to her sisters, a few of which have recently turned up. They are worth quoting as her interest and enjoyment in everything comes through. Her first card reads: "I write while we wait at the airport for the plane which is to take us to Malaga. We have been in Madrid less than a day but long enough to have lost our hearts to the Ritz, the nicest hotel I have ever been in. The dinner the best I have had in years. Francesca and Ros have joined us and are very gay, the perfect traveling companions. We get back to Madrid and the Prado in about two weeks. Lovely weather, very warm. E."

We had arranged to have a car and driver meet us at

Malaga and we started the next day on that beautiful trip to Granada. Edith loved motoring and she could drive for hours on end without fatigue. Our Granada hotel was superbly situated, looking over a deep valley to the Sierra mountains. The Alhambra was within easy walking distance and we spent many hours there.

In a card from Ubeda, Edith wrote, "This is an enchanting town back in the middle ages. We left Granada this morning regretfully. It is more than the height of prettiness; it is lovely. The weather is perfect."

We were heading for Seville and spending the second night at Cordoba. But none of the cards she sent on this part of our trip has been found. The next card I have says:

"We left Seville Saturday morning and stayed the night at this place [Caceres], a tiny town on the top of a little hill and unbelievably medieval and charming, and flower bedecked. No postcards of them. The next day, yesterday, we went up to Guadalupe, but the Virgin was a poor show compared to Seville's and I did not care to go and look at her jewelry. But we stepped out of the church into a dining room—part of the church—where we had a most amusing lunch served by nuns with a lot of priests often smoking cigarettes and helping the nuns. They were a jolly laughing lot. Peals of laughter especially at one priest."

We spent about two weeks in Madrid taking excursions to Avila, Segovia, Toledo, and elsewhere. Edith's especial joy was the Prado. One could go out of the back door of the Ritz Hotel and just step across the street into the gallery. Many times she would slip away from us and if we wanted to find her we knew she would be somewhere in the Prado.

Two cards from Toledo read, "Here is your favorite city as we caught the first glimpse of it yesterday. It rivals Granada and that is much for me to say. I went twice to the Cathedral and sat in it for awhile. And I saw two El Grecos that have made him my con-cordium painter." "Another of Toledo for you. We drove down streets where the people stood back in doorways to let us pass and walked down others where three people could not go abreast. It was a wonderful day. We left here at ten and got back around seven. I have been quiet today just going to see the wonderful Goyas around the dome of a tiny church."

From Segovia she wrote of the Alcazar. "This is a castle in a fairystory—a Spanish story. I am not sending you the Aqueduct for all the pictures of it are poor, but I felt thrilled by the Romans when I looked at it."

In a card from Avila she wrote, "Avila really seems to outdo Carcassonne. The drive was beautiful with some snowy mountains. We turned aside on the way back to see the Escorial. What a place—drearily commonplace except for its size which is wholly a drawback. I did not go in. I don't think I shall."

Shortly before we left Madrid the American ambassador, John Lodge, whose mother was a great friend of Edith's, gave her a big lunch. Edith wrote of it. "The

Embassy lunch was a grand affair, twenty to thirty people, but very pleasant. I found out from John where I could see the best Flamenco dancing."

We went to a large hall where the dancing started at eight-thirty. Edith was so enthralled with it that she stayed there absorbed until after two A.M.

The last postcard I have reads, "This is almost the end of a perfect month. Tomorrow we fly to Cambridge to spend a few days with George, then home by boat." We were visiting a very old friend, Sir George Thomson, who was then master of Corpus Christi. After a short but delightful visit we came home by boat.

The next summer the National Broadcasting Company asked Edith if she would be the guest on their television show, *Wisdom*. Mr. Ginna, the producer, after visiting Edith at Sea Wall, said he would like to take the picture on our rocks rather than in a studio. He discussed at length who would be the best person for her "interviewer." When he mentioned Huntington Cairns, Edith said that he would be her first choice but he was at his summer place at Kitty Hawk, North Carolina, and she would not think of asking him to make the long journey to Maine. Mr. Ginna said that he would go down to Kitty Hawk and talk over the proposition with him. Then Edith got agitated. Would Mr. Ginna promise not to make Mr. Cairns feel he ought to come? Would he promise not to tell him that she had said how much she would like to have him? Mr. Ginna promised, but I doubt if he kept to that agreement. In any case,

Mr. Cairns said he would certainly make the trip to Sea
Wall and a date was set for recording the interview.

Neither Edith nor I had the faintest idea of what the
production of such a television program involved. She
was told that on a certain morning they would "shoot"
the picture on the rocks at about 11:30 A.M. She had
visualized one or two men with cameras. When she
looked out of her window that morning she saw two gigantic trucks with men struggling with various pieces of
equipment, and six or seven automobiles filled with more
men. Another truck rolled up from the electric company, which had been asked to put a cable from the
house down to the rocks, a distance of about a hundred
yards. The whole place, back and front, was a mad-
house.

When 11:30 arrived and Edith and Huntington left
the house, our lonely ocean rocks looked like the
World's Fair before the buildings had been completed.
Edith said to Huntington, "*How* can we concentrate in
the midst of that bedlam? Well, I must force myself to
disregard it." The tide was coming in and was almost
high. A wave would break and one could not hear a
word Edith was saying. They would wait a moment and
have her say it all over again. It finally became impossible, and Mr. Ginna told Huntington to say something
about the tide, get up from the rocks on which they
were sitting, give his hand to Edith to help her up, and
then walk with her toward the house. Huntington said,
"It will take two men to get me off this boulder. Miss

Hamilton will just jump up!"

The plan was to finish the program on our porch. It took them six hours to move the equipment up to the house and it was decided to put off taking the next pictures until the following day. That morning Edith put on a different dress and when she arrived on the porch Mr. Ginna exclaimed, "*Miss Hamilton,* don't you realize that when this show is given it will look as if you had walked from the rocks to the porch and went right on talking. You could hardly have changed your dress on the way up!" "No, I haven't an idea of what you are all doing," said Edith, laughing, as she went back to put on the other dress.

A week or so before the National Broadcasting Company arrived Edith had speculated on about how long it would take them to make the picture. As the program was to be half an hour she decided that they could not take more than an hour and a half. They were there two nights and three days. They had a crew of about twenty men, who were all over the house and place. The trucks arrived early each morning and twice, when making the sharp turn from the main road to ours, they ran over and broke our water pipe, thereby cutting off the water from our house and four others.

Edith and Huntington talked together off and on for two hours and fifty minutes by the clock. That Mr. Ginna picked out, condensed, and made a consecutive thirty-minute whole out of all this is a great tribute to his talents.

The twenty men could not possibly have been nicer and gave Edith much amusement. She asked one of them if he was connected with the sound equipment and he told her that he was not connected with anything at all. "They picked me up in Ellsworth," he said, "because the union required the National Broadcasting Company to have another man on their crew. I am getting twenty-five dollars a day to sit around looking at your lovely view."

There was one man whom we could not quite place. Edith declared that whenever she walked out of the house he appeared from behind a bush or "some other unlikely spot" and snapped a picture with his camera. As a matter of fact, he got some excellent pictures of her, which subsequently appeared in various magazines.

The second evening the men had a cookout on our rocks. It was clear that they were not accustomed to this form of diversion, for they lit the fire with damp seaweed and the resultant huge cloud of smoke which went up into the sky and was visible for a mile around led the fire department to call up and ask if we needed their help.

These three days were to Edith a surprising, wholly novel, and entertaining experience.

The following winter the National Broadcasting Company gave a preview of the performance at a hall in Rockefeller Plaza. Curiosity as to what was made out of the mad confusion at Sea Wall, and also the urging of friends, led us to go to New York and see it. The hall was packed. The picture was thrown on a huge screen, and it was truly excellent. Edith said over and over again, "Mr. Ginna must be a genius." The television show was a great success and is still being repeated at various places throughout the country.

Edith had been working steadily on the Plato's "complete works" project. Choosing the various translations was a more time-consuming task than she had anticipated. Once she was studying three different translations of the same Dialogue and I remember her throwing them down on the sofa and saying, "I am in despair. I will settle on, say, a number-one translation, then see that number two renders certain parts better, and then find that several paragraphs are done best of all in number three. I can't pick out bits from each of them, now can I?"

Shortly thereafter, Huntington brought an editor of the Bollingen to call on her in Washington. He expressed great enthusiasm for what she had written, but Edith sensed that he was leading up to some criticism and she said:

"Now do make me some suggestions."

"Well you see, Miss Hamilton, in pointing out the essence of each of the Dialogues in your excellent introductions, you occasionally translate a line or so from the original text. Then the reader, who presumably goes on to read the given translation of that Dialogue, finds that the line you have quoted is not there. The idea may be, but the words you use are not."

"Oh! I have translated those important lines my-self."

"But you can't do that. You have selected a certain translation and if you 'quote' you must quote from that. It would be very confusing to the reader otherwise. See what I mean?" Edith saw.

"Oh dear!" she exclaimed. "Of course you are right. But those few quotes I have given are not done well in any of the translations." After some discussion it was decided that she would paraphrase her quotations. "Isn't this all too tiresome!" she said with a sigh.

In the spring of 1960 the renowned German classicist, Werner Jaeger, came to Washington and a luncheon was given for him and Edith. I was also invited, and when they were introduced he pulled out of his pocket a much-worn newspaper clipping and said, "Miss Hamilton, do you remember the first sentence of your review of my *Paideia* in *The New York Times* of 1945?" My heart sank. What *had* she said? Her ability to write exceedingly witty adverse comments was well known. He handed the clipping to Edith and she read aloud, "This is the most illuminating book that I have ever read on Greece." It was hardly necessary to say that they had a very pleasant lunch together! And then it came back to my mind that Edith always had a particular admiration for Professor Jaeger and his approach to ancient Greece.

Shortly after Edith's ninety-second birthday we were called upon by an English actress who was putting on Edith's translation of the *Agamemnon* of Aeschylus.

She wanted to know if Edith could be persuaded to translate the rest of the *Oresteia*. "No," said Edith, and then added, "I am saving translating for my old age." She said this with a smile but she meant it, and in the presence of her extraordinary power and vitality of mind and body her remark somehow seemed quite reasonable.

The *Oresteia* was given in London with great success, and the reviewers all said how much finer the translation of the *Agamemnon* was than that of the other two plays of the trilogy. Edith maintained, however, with deep conviction, that the *Agamemnon* was much the greatest of the three plays. "That is why," she said, "I did not translate the other two and I am never going to."

Early in June of 1960 we flew to Paris, where Francesca Palmer and Dorna McCollester joined us and we took a three-week motor trip through France. It was, as were all our travels, unalloyed pleasure. We went first to Chartres and then motored south as far as Aigues Mortes. Edith often repeated the two lines in Macaulay's "Ivry," "Through thy cornfields green, and sunny vines, oh pleasant land of France!" It was just that. We had a particularly stunning drive through the Gorge de Tarn and spent the night at the Château La Malene surrounded by cliffs and gorges.

We went to Loches, Les Eyzies, Nîmes, Arles, Les Baux, and Villeneuve-lès-Avignon, which especially lovely. In the past Edith had been to all these

places but she said she had never seen the Lake of An-
necy and had always wanted to. So we spent a night at
Talloires, which was almost in the lake. It is an incredibly beautiful spot.

We ended our trip back in Paris, where we stayed
for several days, and flew home on July first with the
Sea Wall summer ahead of us.

In January, 1961, Edith received a long telegram
signed President Elect and Mrs. Kennedy. It said that the
forthcoming Administration would "seek a productive
relationship" with its writers, artists, heads of cultural in-
stitutions, etc. Edith was most cordially invited to attend
the inaugural ceremonies on January 19 and 20. Reservations for the inaugural concert, parade, and ball were
being held for her. R.S.V.P. was requested as to which
events she would attend. Edith was highly amused. She
never went to any such public functions.

We watched the inaugural parade over the television.
A picture of a large reserved box was thrown on the
screen several times filled with what Edith called "the
important 'cultured' of the country." "How thankful I
am not to be there," she said. "Wouldn't it be deadly?"

Washington had acquired some acres of land on
which to develop a "cultural center." Edith received
notes from President Kennedy and Mrs. Kennedy asking
her please to receive a gentleman who would call on her
and explain the project in detail and get her reactions to
it. The gentleman came to see her in Maine, bringing a
number of blueprints showing the plans for the various

buildings, the concert hall, theatres, opera house, and others. He explained carefully how they had worked out the approach to the "center" and the entrances that would make it most convenient.

When he finished this discourse Edith said, "But you have told me about nothing except buildings. What is going to take place inside them?" "The National Symphony Orchestra will of course play in the concert hall," he replied. "It has been playing successfully for years in Constitution Hall," Edith answered. The conversation continued.

"Well now, Miss Hamilton, you must admit that the theatre in Washington doesn't amount to much—it is almost negligible."

"I doubt if the theatre buildings are responsible for that."

"Why do you think that there is so little theatre, so few plays in your city?"

"I haven't the least idea. Now don't misunderstand me. I am in no way decrying the idea of a cultural center. It is just that I have little interest in such projects. That is one of my great limitations." Edith stopped, laughed, and said, "I expect we must face the fact that you have come to the wrong person."

During 1960–61 Edith gave four public lectures. One was at the Greek Orthodox Church in Washington. It was to be given one evening in the lecture hall of the church but the audience was so large that the young priest who was in charge told Edith that he was moving it into the church proper. "But I have no hat on," Edith objected. "That makes no difference," he answered, surprisingly, "but I will have to say in introducing you that we can't have any clapping in the church." He was obeyed, and when Edith moved to the desk the entire congregation rose silently to its feet. Afterward many of us were taken downstairs to a hall where sandwiches and coffee were served and the young priest made a delightful host. Edith could not get over it. She kept saying, "That was not like the Greek Orthodox Church as I remember it."

Edith also lectured at the Church of St. John. Then the Classical Association of the Atlantic States held its annual meeting in Washington and again John Latimer asked her to give the address. On April 26, 1960, there was to be a big dinner after which she was to talk, but on the night of the twenty-third she tripped over a rug, fell crashing onto the edge of a table, and broke her nose. I was able to get a surgeon that evening who took care of things, stopped the bleeding, and said that he did not think her nose need be reset. He then told her that she could not possibly make that speech on the twenty-sixth, that she was bound to have a reaction to such a severe shock, and that she should plan to spend the next few days in bed. Realizing that he was making no impression on her whatever, he changed his tactics and said, "Do you know what you are going to look like Miss Hamilton? You will be black and blue from the top of your head to your chin." She was.

It is hardly necessary to say that she gave her lecture. The next day the *Washington Post* published a picture of her with big headlines: "Noted Greek Scholar at 92 Shows She's a Real Spartan." It went on to say, "Edith Hamilton kept a speaking engagement last night in spite of a broken nose." Mr. Latimer, in introducing her, spoke of her accident and in acknowledging his remarks she said, "I thank you for a new experience always earnestly sought for at my age. I had never been to a beauty parlor before. Then I broke my nose and became a perfect spectacle. You would never know it but I am all colors of the rainbow." The beauty parlor had certainly done a marvelous "cover up" job!

The subject of her talk was Plato. It was her custom, when delivering a lecture, to write it out with great care, after which she knew it by heart and would throw away the manuscript. By some chance this Plato address and her talk at St. John's church escaped the scrap basket and were published after her death in her collected essays, *The Ever-Present Past*. In the autumn, she made her speech at the Bryn Mawr School's 75th Anniversary.

During this year she wrote a radio address for the Voice of America "Roots of Freedom" Series, also published in *The Ever-Present Past*.

In the spring of 1961 we had planned another trip abroad. We were going by boat to the Hague, where Mrs. Palmer and Mrs. McCollester were to join us. Then we four were to take a motor trip through Holland, Germany, and into Switzerland.

Edith planned to spend a week at Hadlyme with her sisters before we sailed, and the night she was to leave Washington, Margaret telephoned to say that Alice had been rushed to the hospital in a serious condition. Alice was then over ninety years old and Edith said immediately, as I knew she would, that we must cancel our passage on the boat and all our reservations abroad and cable Francesca and Dorna, who had flown over ahead of us. All this was done. Edith spent some time at Hadlyme and Alice made a remarkable recovery.

Ave atque vale

That autumn the Plato collected works was published. Edith went over it with considerable satisfaction. The book was not as big and cumbersome as she had thought it would surely be, and she was delighted with Huntington Cairns' introduction. She read over her own introductions to the Dialogues and often remarked: "Oh dear! I could have done that much better. Now I must finish my book on Plato. I have completed all the work for it."

Then suddenly, unexpectedly, with no warning whatever, Edith had a stroke. She was very ill indeed and it looked as though the end had come. She was apparently in a coma when a doctor said to me: "You must face the fact that Miss Hamilton will never walk again and never talk again." Edith opened her eyes, looked up, and murmured: "Pooh!"

And "pooh" it was. Her recovery was a miracle. We spent the following summer at Sea Wall as usual. It had been our custom for years to have a party on her birthday, August 12. It was attended first by Dorian and his sisters, then came the grandnieces and nephews. Her sister Alice always came up for the occasion, and anybody else who was visiting us at the time was present. This summer was Edith's ninety-fifth birthday and, in addition to the family, her good friends, the Alan Valentines, came over from North Haven to celebrate.

A week before she died, on May 31, 1963, she seemed to have regained some of her keenness. She said to me: "You know I haven't felt up to writing but now I think I am going to be able to finish that book on Plato." This was completely in character. She always looked to the future. Shortly thereafter she just stopped breathing. She died as she had lived.

John Mason Brown in his article "The Heritage of Edith Hamilton" (*Saturday Review*, June 22, 1963) wrote:

"When she died three weeks ago at ninety-five, Edith Hamilton was unquestionably aged but remained ageless. She was as old in the wisdom of which she was the embodiment as she was young in her relish of today's trivia and gossip . . . she was as much at home in our worlds as she was in ancient Greece or Rome."

Later on in this same article he wrote:

"Nobility of mind, character, and spirit is rare indeed. Wisdom, true wisdom, is no less rare. Edith, one of the most human of mortals was the radiant possessor of both."

Her Writings

The Dust of Centuries

❧ THE importance of ancient Greece has been "softly
dimmed by the dust of centuries of scholarly elucida-
tion." So wrote Edith in her first book, *The Greek Way.*
That sentence has been referred to many times in praise
and in rage. It put into a few words her attitude toward
many scholarly treatises. This attitude is expressed in
one way or another in every book she wrote. She believed that "the writings of the day show the quality
of the people as no historical reconstruction can."

This deep conviction explains why her scholarship
led to her absorption in one thing alone, the writings and
literature of the age. "A people's literature is the great
textbook for real knowledge of them," she wrote in her
introduction to *The Roman Way.* She states that in this
book she will consider Rome entirely as it is marked out
by Roman writers. "It is in no sense a history of Rome."
In her first chapter, "Comedy's Mirror," she discusses at
length Plautus and Terence, as they draw the first picture we have of Rome. They wrote a series of comedies
avowedly founded on the popular Greek comedy of the
day, and there have been centuries of debate between the

scholars, she tells us, as to whether or not these plays were direct copies of the Greek. She writes that the "essential quality of a comic play" precluded the theory that they were not Roman products.

"Those who argue that they gave their audiences not Rome but Greece, foreign folk whose ways were strange to Romans, do not take into account the nature of comedy. It must present the familiar. An easy understanding of what is going on is essential. Let puzzlement or what follows inevitably in its train, disapproval, come in and comedy is at an end. The audience are not there to have their minds enlarged geographically or ethnologically. They want to see people they know about and life lived in the way they live it. A stray foreigner acting according to his own foolish foreign notions is a capital figure of fun, but a stage peopled with such would not be funny at all."

Of Menander she writes, "The question how closely they [the Romans] imitated the Greek New Comedy, to what degree they translated or followed their own genius, is one to delight the scholarly mind because it never can be settled by scholarly standards. The battle of the learned can be waged forever. Too little is left of Menander's work for even the most erudite to give the victory on that score to either side, and of his fellow-comedians nothing is left at all."

Comedy to be comedy must present the familiar. The last paragraph of the chapter "Comedy's Mirror" reads as follows: "Theories that go counter to the facts of human nature are foredoomed. Comedy in Rome to be comedy had of necessity to be Roman and no argument, linguistical, historical, archaeological, can have any counterbalancing weight against this fundamental truth. The mirror of Plautus and Terence reflects not a strange, shadowy Greece, but their own day and their own city, the veritable Rome of the Republic."

She dismissed many scholarly assumptions. This is shown most clearly in her essay "The Greek Chorus," which begins, "When I was a girl at college I was taught a neat and simple scheme which comprised within itself all that one need to know about the externals of the Greek tragic drama: three actors made up the full complement for every play; each actor was raised above the ground by means of a cothurnus or boot which had a short pillar attached to the sole; and finally the chorus always numbered fifteen. These dogmas were taught precisely as if they had come down in a book written on stage technique in the fifth century B.C."

Edith decided that these rules were impossible. If there were only three actors in each play, she knew that in the *Oedipus Coloneus*, for instance, one of the parts would have to be shifted back and forth four times. In one of the plays the king's boots are removed and clearly he would suddenly become a head shorter than the others on the stage. "As for the invariable chorus of fifteen," she wrote, "the only Greek play which mentions the number of the chorus, the *Suppliants* of Aeschylus, refers to it always as fifty."

Her essay continues: "Undoubtedly these [rules] were troubles, but they were not taken seriously. To do so would have involved looking at the plays as theatrical productions and that was never done. The scholars who established these dogmas of the Athenian stage were men of the library, not the theatre. They had deep learning and keen scholarly acumen; they tracked down every allusion in literature that might bear upon the matter; they deciphered old manuscripts and clarified old inscriptions. But they paid no attention to the fact that the subject of their study was, in the final analysis, a dramatic performance, and they never stopped to consider the rules and regulations they laid down so authoritatively for the tremendous living force which all great drama is.

"No one else ever stopped to consider it either. Dogmas are so comfortable. One can rest in perfect peace on ex cathedra utterances delivered securely from the lecture platform and taken down accurately in notebooks."

She went on to say, "People are theatre-conscious today as in no other age and, as a result, Greek tragedy has been brought out of the library on to the boards. The cothurnus and the three-actor rule have both been considered under a new aspect, their theatrical practicability. From this point of view it becomes instantly apparent that the idea of an important role being changed four times back and forth between different actors, to the entire satisfaction of the Athenian audience, is more difficult to credit than the occasional infringement of the scholars' rule of three. It is true that this conclusion does away with all the careful diagrams, as delightfully complicated as any jig-saw puzzle, which proved that three actors were factually possible, but it also restores the Athenians to the position of alert spectators, which seems no more than their due.

"In the same way the old solution for those troublesome high boots of Agamemnon's—that the attendants did not pull them off, but merely pretended to do so, rested upon the assumption of a childlike naïveté on the part of the audience, who allowed the imposture and contentedly watched the king clump along on his pillars over the purple he had just declared no boot should ever touch. The cothurnus, too, has had to retreat before dramatic probability.

"But so far the rule of fifteen for the chorus has not been called into serious question. [This is still the case in 1967.] The theatrical difficulty involved in it presented itself first to my mind when I was shown pictures of the performances of the *Prometheus* at Delphi. The tiny band of fifteen appeared ludicrously inadequate on that great orchestra surrounded by the immense auditorium with the mighty cliffs of the mountains towering above. Again it came to me with an even sharper perception when I stood in the theatre at Epidaurus, looking up to the endless tiers of seats and down to the enormous circle of the dancing floor. Fifteen performers on so vast a stage, so far removed from the spectators—and the Greeks with their sure sense of proportion in beauty. I could not bring the two ideas together. Then and there I determined to find out what was the basis for the dogma, why every writer on the subject declared that in the great age of the Athenian stage the number was fifteen."

Although, since college days, Edith was quite familiar with the ancient authorities and their assertions, she decided she would go into the matter more thoroughly, and she gathered and examined all the evidence for the rule of fifteen. "The authorities," she wrote, "look impressive; the scholiasts on a passage in the *Birds*, the *Eumenides*, and the *Knights*; the anonymous *Life of Aeschylus*; Pollux; Photion, Tzetzes; Suidas. The array appears to the casual and even to the careful reader quite decisive. But a closer investigation brings doubts."

She then gives us a detailed account of what each one of them said, how they disagreed on many points and the complete lack of evidence they had for some of their conclusions. She points out that the earliest of these authorities lived some seven hundred years after the plays were given. She says that if we must have a rule for the number in the chorus, fifty would be more justified than fifteen. "But why should there be such a rule?" she concludes. "The only possible reason for supposing that the size of the chorus was always the same is that the great orchestra demanded a large body of dancers and that the Athenians were used to fifty. But shall we then follow the procedure of the scholars in their libraries and declare that although in Euripides' *Suppliants* the chorus is stated to be seven women with their handmaidens, it must, according to our rule, have numbered fifty? Wider knowledge brings less certainty, a more open mind, an undogmatic attitude. We shall do better to acknowledge that we have no reason whatever to feel sure about the number of the early chorus. We may, however, feel sure of one thing: that men like Aeschylus, Sophocles, Euripides, always use their materials as they choose; they are never dictated to by them. If we disengage our minds from ascribing to them a rigid adherence to petty regulations, we shall find ourselves more able to understand the power that produced Greek tragedy."

She found interest and enjoyment in some of the debates and theories on matters that could "never be settled by scholarly standards." I think she considered them a sort of indoor sport. At best they were of no great importance. Speaking of Plato's Dialogues, she referred in a lecture to the hundreds of years of debate that has never been settled as to whether Socrates was a creation of Plato's or a portrait from life, and she said, "However that may be, the picture we are left with is extraordinarily vivid and impressive, and to the reader today it is apt to seem unimportant how much of Socrates is Plato and how much of Plato is Socrates."

In her introduction to *Mythology* she says that Greek and Roman mythology are quite generally supposed to show us the way the human race thought and felt in prehistoric days. She says that we do not know when the mythological stories were first told in their present shape, "but whenever it was, primitive life had been left far behind." She writes, "Nothing is clearer than the fact that primitive man, whether in New Guinea today or eons ago in the prehistoric wilderness, is not and never has been a creature who peoples his world with bright fancies. Horrors lurk in the primeval forest, not nymphs and naiads. Terror lived there, with its close attendant, magic, and its most common defence, human sacrifice. . . . Only a few traces of that time are to be found in the stories." She points out that the first written record of Greece is the *Iliad*, "which is, or contains, the oldest Greek literature; and it is written in a rich and subtle and beautiful language which must have had behind it centuries when men were striving to express themselves with clarity and beauty, an indisputable proof of civilization. . . . The study of the way early man looked at his surroundings does not get much help from the Greeks. How briefly the anthropologists treat the Greek myths is noteworthy."

The same original approach to her conclusions is expressed in her introduction to her translation of the *Prometheus*. She writes: "Ocean's character merits a fuller consideration for the reason that the traditional view is that Attic tragedy did not admit of comedy or humor. The text books all tell us that it was unrelieved by any lighter touch, and so gained an intensity of tragic effect. . . . But most readers will agree that the comedy of Ocean's talk with Prometheus is beyond dispute. Ocean is a humorous creation, an amiable self-important old busybody, really distressed at Prometheus' hard fate, but bent upon reading him a good lecture now that he has him where he cannot run away; delighted to find himself the person of importance who has pull with Zeus and can get that unpractical fool, Prometheus, out of his not entirely undeserved punishment; but underneath his superior attitude very uneasy because of Zeus, who 'isn't so far off but he might hear,' and completely happy when Prometheus finally gives him a chance to save his face and run off safely home. When this dialogue is understood as humorous, the commentators and translators are relieved of what had always been a stumbling block to them, Ocean's four-footed bird. If it is accepted as axiomatic that a Greek tragic drama cannot have anything humorous in it, the bird with four feet undoubtedly presents difficulties. It is hard to see it as a tragic adjunct. But the Athenian spectators were at least as keen-witted as we are today, and when there appeared on the stage an enormous bird with a pompous old man riding on its back, they had no more trouble than we should have in recognizing a comic interlude. Ocean is a figure of fun, and the steed he bestrides is there to give the audience the clue."

These quotations are indicative of her method of arriving at her conclusions.

This is clearly shown in the last paragraph of "Comedy's Mirror." In drawing her conclusions, Edith dismisses the "linguistical, historical, archaeological." Her concern is "the nature of Comedy" and there are no "ifs," "ands," or "buts" or "it seems to me's" in what she writes. Edith was not expressing her opinion, she was simply pointing out a fundamental truth.

Again, in her conclusion to the chapter "The Greek Chorus," after giving all the evidence for the fifteen-in-the-chorus belief, she makes a flat statement that "we have no reason whatever to feel sure about the number of the early chorus." She did not consider that she was expressing an opinion, she was stating a fact.

There were some students who said that Edith was not a scholar, that she was "just" a popularizer. What is the definition of a scholar? If one means by that word a person of real ability who has studied a subject over many years and knows it as few could better, Edith was certainly a scholar. If one means by a "scholar" one whose books would not be read except by another student in the same line, then Edith was not a scholar. Furthermore, her approach to her subject and her reasons for arriving at her conclusions were her own and unlike those of the conventional scholar.

If Edith made lighthearted jibes at some scholarly preoccupations, a few of the erudite did not find her remarks so amusing, and were not prepared to pass them by.

Early in her writing career she received a critical letter from an English classicist. It was interspersed with laudatory remarks but, to Edith, the essence of it was that she had written an unscholarly idealization of ancient Greece; that she had either failed to recognize or chose to ignore the many undesirable customs in that civilization; that although her praise of the tragedians was wholly justified, she had not mentioned the poor lines that also appeared in these plays.

In spite of her great popularity, or perhaps because of it, there were those who enjoyed making comments along these lines. Edith was sensitive to such attacks but it was not the specific points made that bothered her. It was that anyone could make her feel that she had failed to get her points across, or, in short, that her book was not very good.

No one and nothing, however, could shake her profound convictions. She believed, among other things, that in dealing with the truly great—poets, musicians, writers, painters, thinkers—it was their best works that mattered and their inferior productions were of no importance. She wrote, "We never think of the poor lines Shakespeare could write, or the terrible verses Wordsworth sometimes perpetrated. None of that matters. People who achieve greatness anywhere, in anything, are remembered for that. The rest of them is dropped out of sight." The Greeks, she wrote, "left behind a record in art and thought which all the centuries of human effort since has not surpassed." Even her most carping critics did not dispute the validity of her statement. This remarkable achievement, she said, was certainly not made on account of their faults. These were of no lasting importance. She "dropped them out of sight."

The object of *The Greek Way* was to present and explain why "we think and feel differently because of

what a little Greek town did during a century or two
twenty-four hundred years ago." She states that she was
not writing a history of Greece.

The Greek Way, published in 1930, immediately
fired the imagination of both scholars and general readers. It brought fifth-century Athens to life for many
people. One highly intelligent woman told me that when
she had graduated from college all she knew of ancient
Greece was terra cotta vases with black figures going
in two different directions at the same time. *The Greek
Way*, she said, opened up a whole new world for her. It
was said that Edith's book started the ever-growing interest in ancient Greece which has been evident over the
last years.

Rosamond Gilder, who became dramatic critic and
later the editor of the *Theatre Arts Monthly* and is now
president of the International Theatre Institute, wrote
the following about Edith: "We learned from her that
Aeschylus, Sophocles, Euripides and Aristophanes were
indeed the source not only of inspiration but of information. These texts contain not only the great dramatic
poetry that launched the Western Theatre, but provide
most of the authentic information we have on the contemporary playwrights, actors, choruses and audiences
of the Great Age—far more so than later commentators.

"As Edith read aloud from the Greek texts, the theatre came to life for us in a way that volumes of learned
commentary had never succeeded in doing."

C. M. Bowra, Oxford's distinguished Greek scholar, wrote of her in 1964, "Her book *The Greek Way* is the authentic utterance of one who lived so long in her imagination with the Greeks that she made them part of herself and formed an intimacy with them which few more strictly professional scholars could attain. She wrote of them with the special understanding which comes from single-minded devotion and admiring affection. Her ideas were emphatically her own, and though she inevitably owed something to other scholars, everything she said had her own imprint on it and rose from her unflagging concern for what the Greeks did and said and were.

"Miss Hamilton started from the best, the right, the only possible point—the actual texts of Greek literature," Bowra continues. "Yet she tempered this remarkable sympathy with a high degree of intelligence and detachment." He writes that the great age of Athens which appealed so strongly to Edith had many faults. He then says, "In the long run, however, what matters is that the Greeks themselves admitted such actions to be wrong and condemned them, and it is from what they themselves said that Miss Hamilton formed her judgment. Her masterly treatment of Thucydides is also a wise commentary on the decline of Athens, her appreciation of Plato sets him both in his historical place as a child of a defeated generation and in his timeless grandeur as one who understood, as few have done, the strange ways by which truth can be elicited from confusion by affection as well as by argument. . . . Miss Hamilton saw beyond the immediate, individual events to wider issues behind them."

Mind and Spirit

A DEEP conviction that Edith expresses in all her books is the difference between the truths of the mind and the truths of the spirit. She wrote, "The bitterest conflicts that have divided the minds of men and set family against family, and brother against brother, have not been waged for emperor or king, but for one side of the truth to the suppression of the other side."

To Edith the truths of the mind and the truths of the spirit although profoundly different were both true. It was one reason for her great love for fifth-century Athens. She wrote, "The flowering of genius in Greece was due to the immense impetus given when clarity and power of thought was added to great spiritual force. . . . The spirit of inquiry with the spirit of poetry . . . It made the Athenians lovers of fact and of beauty; it enabled them to hold fast both to the things that are seen and to the things that are not seen, in all they have left behind for us, science, philosophy, religion, art."

This is a major theme in *The Greek Way*. The book ends with the following paragraph:

"For a hundred years Athens was a city where the great spiritual forces that war in men's minds flowed along together in peace; law and freedom, truth and religion, beauty and goodness, the objective and the subjective—there was a truce to their eternal warfare, and the result was the balance and clarity, the harmony and completeness, the word Greek has come to stand for. They saw both sides of the paradox of truth, giving predominance to neither, and in all Greek art there is an absence of struggle, a reconciling power, something of calm and serenity, the world has yet to see again."

John Mason Brown wrote of her, "Although she wrote brilliantly about St. Paul, beautifully about Jesus, revealingly of the prophets of Israel, with deep knowledge of the outstanding Romans, and with particular charm about Horace, Greece was the love of Edith's life."

Edith found fifth-century Athens a unique combination of the qualities that she herself, in her own degree, possessed—mind and spirit, intellect and art. She said that we are so familiar with Greek art that we are apt to forget that they were the first intellectualists. In her own words: "The Greeks were the first scientists and all science goes back to them."

The Greeks' power of clear, unmuddled thinking appealed greatly to Edith. It banished sentimentality. She wrote, "They were not tempted to evade facts. It is we ourselves who are the sentimentalists. We, to whom poetry, all art, is only a superficial decoration of life, make a refuge from a world that is too hard for us to face by sentimentalizing it. The Greeks looked straight at it. They were completely unsentimental. It was a

Roman who said it was sweet to die for one's country. The Greeks never said it was sweet to die for anything. They had no vital lies."

In her essay on Faulkner Edith writes, "In the past, a determination not to be dominated by fact, led persistently to the land of heart's desire where everyone and everything was good and true and beautiful. Now it leads to just the opposite, where nothing is good or true or beautiful. Of course one is just as much an escape as the other. It is just as far from reality to shut out all that is agreeable. Both extremes are equally unreal, and both are equally romantic. . . . The danger to the romantic, equally present whether he turns his back on ugliness or on loveliness, is sentimentality. It is easily recognized in the first case, but not in the second. There is a general impression that to describe things as dull and drab and unpleasant is realism and farthest removed from the roses and raptures of sentimentality. That is not true. The extremely unpleasant can be extremely sentimental. Sentimentality is always false sentiment. It is such a danger to the romantic artist because he has escaped from the domination of fact, and sentimentality is falsehood to fact.

"When Edgar Lee Masters described a baby:

> 'She was some kind of crying thing
> One takes in one's arms and all at once
> It slimes your face with its running nose,
> And voids its essence all over you,
> And there you stand smelling to heaven—'

he has fallen into one extreme of sentimental unreality as truly as Swinburne has into the other when he writes:

'A baby's eyes—
Their glance might cast out pain and sin,
Their speech make dumb the wise,
By mute glad god-head felt within
A baby's eyes.'

"Neither Masters nor Swinburne, of course, was in the least concerned with what a baby is really like. They had escaped from that limitation. Perhaps each in his way was seeking for some other truth than the truth of nature, but all we know is that the result was falsehood for both of them, pure sentimentality, as much in the case of the nasty baby as in the case of the baby with the momentous eyes."

The Greeks' longing for the light of reason and for truth banished sentimentality.

Edith's writings often reveal a sharp and witty intellect. But they show beyond all question of doubt that her fundamental absorption was with the things of the spirit.

Her chapters in *The Greek Way* entitled "East and West" and "Mind and Spirit" illuminate the vast difference between the truths of the mind and the truths of the spirit, and the importance of both in our never-ending struggle to reach an answer. The chapter "Faith" in *Witness to the Truth* brings out so vividly what she believes happens when an attempt is made to prove the things of the spirit by the processes of the mind that I quote it in full:

"The power of Christianity, the power of all religion, is sustained by that strange capacity in us we call faith, a word very commonly used and very commonly misunderstood.

"Ages of faith and of unbelief are always said to mark the course of history. The latter part of the nineteenth century with the emergence of modern science is the usual example of an age of unbelief. For the perfect example of an age of faith people have always been told, and are being told today with especial insistence, they must look back to the mediaeval days. Of course it is beyond question that during the middle ages religion was very powerful, indeed supremely powerful; but there is a question whether the kind of religion that flourished then was such as to stamp the times as an age of faith. Certainly, the underlying motive which made many men profess religion had nothing to do with faith. It was fear, which is at the farthest remove from faith. There was a horrible place called hell, as actual as the earth itself, and once in it there was no escape to all eternity. Safety from that horror could be gained only by embracing religion. The idea was that of a perfectly sure and most profitable investment. Life was short, very short, indeed, during those centuries; immortality whether in heaven or hell very long; anyone could see the rationality of foregoing present brief advantage for an endless future profit. The appeal to the crystal-clear superiority of an eternity of bliss to a few years of immediate pleasure is made by the most saintly mediaeval writers; it is found in such masters of the religious life as Thomas à Kempis and John Tauler. It is evident that faith played no part here; it was a mere matter of common sense. Heaven and hell were substantial realities a man could invest in while here below, and no elaborate system of bookkeeping was needed to show which should be crossed out. The so-called Ages of Faith were only Ages of Certainty when men were sure they knew and understood all things in heaven as well as on earth.

"The church claimed to be the source of universal knowledge and her claim was allowed. She was possessed of indisputable information on every subject, not only heaven and hell and the roads that led thither, but the way the world came into being, how the heavenly bodies moved, what was the origin of man (and woman), why different languages arose, and so on, up to the exact constitution of the Holy Trinity. Nothing was as important as to accept these statements. Bliss or misery to all eternity depended upon doing so. How a man acted mattered not at all in comparison. The Inquisition burned people only for thinking incorrectly, not for living unethically.

"During almost all the life of Christianity a wholesale subscription to whatever the church declared to be true was the one thing needful. Faith was something achieved or submitted to by the mind. To have faith in God was to accept what the authorities, men high in the church or learned in the book, asserted was the Truth. Often with a man of spirituality and intellect it came very near to being what the scoffers declared it was, believing what one knew was not so. Religion's chief function was to tell people what to think. It offered men that comforting possession, freedom from all personal responsibility. The mystery of human life was solved; no one need ever be disturbed by it. A neat dogmatic system was provided ready at hand, and to take this as the unalterable measure of the universe was faith.

"It was a state of things which could last only as long as men chose not to question it. A day came when the men of free thought found that the universe was too big for the measure. That is the reason religion had a great setback in the nineteenth century. The church had tied herself up to explanations which were outmoded. When the light of science was turned upon them and they were shown to be false, she and the cause of religion stood discredited. As one after another of the ancient bulwarks, strengthened through centuries of theological thinking, gave way under the assaults of the scientists, the six-day creation, the Garden of Eden, the sun that stopped at the word of the man of God, the toppling down of the whole stupendous structure before astronomy and geology and physics seemed to undermine the foundation of religion. Complacent Christianity had a shattering blow. The theologians had claimed the entire outside universe and they lost it. They had not an inch left in it to stand upon. Ideas for hundreds of years proclaimed as final truth were mere childishness in the new universe that was opening.

"The church had arrogated to herself what did not belong to her. She had insisted that the reason which finds proofs and causes was her own province, and that the field of the mind which observes and organizes facts was indistinguishable from the field of faith. Then the mind and the reason turned against her and she suffered a great defeat.

"She went astray in a matter of supreme importance. She turned faith, without which there is no religion, into something which had no connection with faith. Early in her history her great teachers began to urge it upon the masses as a matter of passive acceptance; upon people disposed to use their minds, as a matter of logical reasoning. The greatest of mediaeval teachers, St. Thomas Aquinas, said he had faith in Christ, first, because Christ had performed miracles, and, second, because he had been foretold by Old Testament prophets. Only third did he place the fact that Christianity taught men how to die. The argument as he saw it was clear: Only God can walk on the water. Christ did so. Therefore Christ is God. This to St. Thomas was the assurance of faith. This was the church's idea of faith when she had to confront modern science.

"But when faith is supported by facts or by logic it ceases to be faith. When factual proof is possible or reasoning from an unquestionable cause to an inevitable effect, faith is excluded. Knowledge leaves no room for faith. When Christ said, 'Blessed are they which have not seen, and yet have believed,' he was describing faith. It belongs to that field of human activity which is concerned with making visible the things that are unseen. The field of faith has a common border with the field of art. That idea never dawned upon the great churchmen, but it would have been well for the church if it had.

"During all the centuries of her life the church has made great use of art, but she has learned nothing from the artists. There was never an artist who did not know that he could not paint his picture or compose his music by thinking out the laws of beauty. If the church had seen the way to her truth as clearly as they did the way to theirs, there would have been no trouble and no defeat. Science never had any quarrel with artistic truth, and the artists never concerned themselves with what the scientists said was true. The painters and the poets and the musicians know that there is an order of reality in which intellectual assurance plays no part and the reason is unimportant. It is not measurable by the machinery of our minds, but it is real. 'All great poetry,' Keats says, 'should produce the instantaneous conviction, this is true.' The function of art, Tolstoi said, is to make that *understood* which in the form of an argument would be incomprehensible. There is a field where all wonderful perfections of microscope and telescope fail, all exquisite niceties of weight and measures, as well as that which is behind them, the keen and driving power of the mind. No facts however indubitably detected, no effort of reason however magnificently maintained, can prove that

Bach's music is beautiful. Keats said of Shakespeare that he saw in him the power of 'resting in uncertainty without any irritable reaching after fact and reason.' What Shakespeare knew, he could not reason out and explain, and that troubled him not at all.

"Definitions and analyses and all such contrivances of the classifying mind were never of any importance to the poets. Aesthetic dogmas might come and go. They never touched poetry. If a man of saintly life disagreed with the churchmen's rules, he suffered, in the so-called Ages of Faith, very painfully indeed. Not so in art. Aristotle's *Poetics* was long the critics' bible, but when Shakespeare was lined up against its rules and came out badly, it was not Shakespeare that suffered, but the rules.

"This has always been the artists' way and therefore their truths are never left behind by the onward march of progress. Time does not touch their knowledge. Aeschylus is not superseded by Shakespeare; the centuries do not diminish Homer. But the truths of the mind are only for a time. They do not endure. They are perpetually cast aside and other truths take their place. Explanations, the very best of them, the highest reaches of the greatest intellects, have a brief life. *'La clarté parfaite, n'est-elle pas le signe de la lassitude des idées?'* The way of the mind is perpetually to doubt and question. Intellectual certainty is hampering. To be sure one understands closes the way to further understanding. But spiritual certainty never stands in the way of greater certainty. The perception of beauty does not hinder the discovery of more beauty. Love does not block the road to more love.

"That final goal of human endeavour, knowledge of the truth, must be sought in many ways. In this world where the scientific truth is 'an aggregation of protons and electrons,' 'a system of interrelated events,' men produce from it an El Greco, the *Oresteia*, the Bach Passion music, an unselfish love, a heroic death. The part our reason can play in our search for truth is limited.

"What the humblest artists knew, the keen minds that contrived the creeds and the catechisms failed to perceive. Perhaps it was not so much a failure in perceiving the truth as a choice which shut the truth out. The able organizers who took hold of the new young life of the Christian Church and bent their powers to defending it from attack and building it up into a mighty fortress superior to attack, demanded something more demonstrable than spiritual certainty, something more substantial than the vision of things not seen and manifested only in imperfect human lives. No solid foundation could be found there for their grand project, to establish in august majesty the great visible Church of God on earth. So they turned to the satisfying and by comparison almost solid ground of reasoned statements and logical deductions. That way one could arrive at something dependable. They produced creeds which were miracles of hairsplitting definitions of the eternal and infinite, and minutely reasoned out 'schemes of salvation' which were clearly demonstrable from premise to conclusion. And very soon faith, which Christ had commanded, but never defined, which St. Paul had said was the power of religion without explaining why, became identified with the explanations and definitions. To know them was to know the truth and to accept them was to have faith.

"This was to make an easy and shallow acquiescence of first importance. It was to elevate believing into a virtue, indeed into the one essential virtue, with the inevitable results of hyprocrisy and self-deception. It was to falsify the foundation upon which Christianity rests.

"Faith is not belief. Belief is passive. Faith is active. It has a driving power. It is vision which passes inevitably into action. 'I have within me,' said Euripides, 'within my soul, a great temple of justice.' That is the only place where justice is. Outside there is nothing but a dim distorted shadow of it. But its unreality in the world does not affect its reality to us nor the passionate protest of our heart when we see injustice. We know what justice is and that it is of first importance. It is real though all the facts say no. To know it thus as true, a truth one will never give up, an idea one will never abandon, is to be halfway on the road to faith in justice. Only halfway; faith is more than conviction. To have faith in justice is not only to perceive what justice is, how great and how excellent, it is also to be constrained to work for its realization, to try to make justice come to pass. Although it does not yet exist faith sees it, and acts to bring it into existence.

"There is one definition of faith in the New Testament, only one, in the Epistle to the Hebrews. It has nothing to do with belief, but entirely with action: 'Now faith is the giving substance to things hoped for, the proving of things not seen.' The way the author substantiates his hope and gives proof of the reality of the unseen is not by a series of statements which are to be accepted, but by marshalling a long list of one life after another, 'a cloud of witnesses,' who so lived that from them men drew patience to run the race set before them. That is always faith's record, lives not creeds. Christ never said, I will tell you the truth, so clearly that you must understand, so convincingly that you must believe. He said, 'I am the truth.' 'His life was the light of men.' Light needs no proof. It needs only to be seen.

"We are so made that we are able to perceive a good which is utterly beyond us and when we see it we must long to do something about it, to have a share in it, if that could be. We needs must love the highest when we see it, and love is always active. Faith in Christ is awareness of his perfection, comprehending the utmost of selfless compassion and love, infinitely past our power to reach, yet insistently driving us to reach it."

Witness to the Truth is a study of the Gospels but it is essentially Edith's portrait of Christ. Apart from the chapter "Faith" it would be impossible to convey her deep convictions by quotation or by any single chapter. The book was and is undoubtedly controversial and many theologians have expressed their strong objections.

But there were other members of the church who had different reactions. Thomas Sugrue, a Roman Catholic, wrote, " A wise and penetrating study of Christ . . . intense, quietly brilliant. It gleams with the substance of learning; it is luminous with understanding and perception." In reviewing the book, Henry Sloane Coffin, a Presbyterian, wrote, "A fresh and most suggestive approach . . . destined for the wide reading it so justly merits." Rufus M. Jones, a Quaker, wrote, "I have read *Witness to the Truth* with tremendous interest and satisfaction. It is an extremely valuable book . . . full of wisdom. . . . It should have a far reaching influence." Charles Haven Myers, a Congregationalist, had this to say, "This beautiful volume is a ray of light upon our dark road."

Now in 1967 the discussion continues with increased intensity. Articles are being published: "Is there a God?"; "God is Dead"; "Who and what is God?" and the like. Edith said in her speech at the church of St. John, "You will search the Gospels in vain for a definition of God. Christ never gave any."

Edith's profound belief in freedom, how the Greeks obtained it, and how they lost it is a major subject in her writings. What is freedom? She wrote, "The creed of the first free government in the world was liberty for all men who could control themselves and would take responsibility for the state."

In a radio address written in 1961 for the Voice of

America "Roots of Freedom" Series she said, "But discovering freedom is not like discovering atomic bombs. It cannot be discovered once for all. If people do not prize it, and work for it, it will depart. Eternal vigilance is its price. Athens changed. It was a change that took place unnoticed though it was of utmost importance, a spiritual change which had penetrated the whole state. It had been the Athenians' pride and joy to give to their city. That they could get material benefits from her never entered their minds. There had to be a complete change of attitude before they could look at the city as an employer who paid her citizens for doing her work. Now instead of men giving to the state, the state was to give to them. What the people wanted was a government which would provide a comfortable life for them; and with this as the foremost object, ideas of freedom and self-reliance and responsibility were obscured to the point of disappearing. Athens was more and more looked on as a co-operative business possessed of great wealth in which all citizens had a right to share.

"She reached the point when the freedom she really wanted was freedom from responsibility. There could be only one result. If men insisted on being free from the burden of self-dependence and responsibility for the common good, they would cease to be free. Responsibility is the price every man must pay for freedom. It is to be had on no other terms. Athens, the Athens of Ancient Greece, refused responsibility; she reached the end of freedom and was never to have it again.

"But, 'the excellent becomes the permanent,' Aristotle said. Athens lost freedom forever, but freedom was not lost forever for the world. A great American statesman, James Madison, in or near 1776 A.D., referred to 'The capacity of mankind for self-government.' No doubt he had not an idea that he was speaking Greek. Athens was not in the farthest background of his mind, but once a great and good idea has dawned upon man, it is never completely lost. The Atomic Age cannot destroy it. Somehow in this or that man's thought such an idea lives though unconsidered by the world of action. One can never be sure that it is not on the point of breaking out into action, only sure that it will do so sometime."

This last paragraph expresses Edith's profound and unshakable belief. She did not think, she knew, that "the excellent becomes the permanent."

In *The Greek Way*, she told of a lecture given by a famous Greek scholar. He was talking about the passage in which the ghosts would not speak to Odysseus until he had given them blood to drink. Then he added, "So, too, the dear ghosts of that departed world will not speak to us unless we give them of our heart's blood." This is what Edith did unstintingly in her writing years.

Her critical essays have given much entertainment and edification, but her lifelong absorption has always been with the great spiritual leaders of mankind. A distinguished man of letters said to me of Edith's books,

"She has a power of presentation, interpretation, and illumination beyond that of any writer I know." Edith said, after describing Thucydides' picture of the Athenians: "Only an ideal? Ideals have enormous power. They stamp an age, they lift up when they are lofty; they drag down and make decadent when they are low—and then, by that strange fact, the survival of the fittest, those that are low fade away and are forgotten. The Greek ideals have had a power of persistent life for twenty-five hundred years."

In the radio program, *This I Believe*, Edith said; "When the world we are living in is storm-driven and the bad that happens and the worse that threatens press urgently upon us, there is a strong tendency to emphasize men's baseness or their impotent insignificance. Is this the way the world is to go or not? It depends upon us.

"St. John spoke of the true light that lighteth every man coming into the world. Belief in the indestructible power of that light makes it indestructible. This lifts up the life of every man to an overwhelming importance and dignity.

"God leaves us free. We are free to choose Him or reject Him. No tremendous miracle will come down from heaven to compel us to accept as a fact a being powerful enough to work it. What would that kind of belief do toward making love or compassion a reality? God puts the truth of Himself into our hands. We must carry the burden of the proof, for His truth can be proved in no other way. 'Glorious is the venture,' Socrates said."

She had said: "The truths of the spirit are proved not by reasoning about them or explanations of them, but only by acting upon them. . . . Lives are the proof of the reality of God."

I think all her readers will agree that her philosophy, her deep and unshakable convictions, come through all her books. They have what Schopenhauer describes as "that singular swing toward elevation."

HONORS AND CITATIONS

HONORARY DEGREES

June 1949 Doctor of Literature, University of Rochester, Rochester, New York

June 1953 Doctor of Literature, University of Pennsylvania, Philadelphia, Pennsylvania

June 1959 Doctor of Literature, Yale University, New Haven, Connecticut

June 1962 Doctor of Laws, Goucher College, Baltimore, Maryland

AWARDS

1951 National Achievement Award, Washington, D.C.

1955 Elected member National Institute of Arts and Letters, New York, New York

1957 Elected member American Academy of Arts and Letters, New York, New York

1957 Gold Cross of the Legion of Benefaction presented by King Paul of Greece
Made Honorary Citizen of Athens
(Both presented in Athens)

1958 Constance Lindsay Skinner Award, New York, New York

1959 Women's National Press Club Award, Washington, D.C.

1960 Award for Distinguished Service, Bryn Mawr College, Pennsylvania

1962 The Jane Addams Medal for Distinguished Service awarded by Rockford College, Rockford, Illinois

1963 Committee formed by the New York Museum of Modern Art voted that "A Conversation with Edith Hamilton" produced on the television in 1959 was the most memorable of the forty WISDOM films made by N.B.C.